Buona Fortuna!
Carole Bradshaw
The Anchor Lady
2010.

FORTUNA

Carole Bradshaw

authorHOUSE®

AuthorHouse™
1663 Liberty Drive
Bloomington, IN 47403
www.authorhouse.com
Phone: 1-800-839-8640

First published by AuthorHouse   2/10/2010

ISBN: 978-1-4490-7084-7 (sc)
ISBN: 978-1-4490-7085-4 (hc)

Printed in the United States of America
Bloomington, Indiana

This book is printed on acid-free paper.

Acknowledgements

For the contributions made by everyone whose lives were touched by the *Fortuna*, thank you.

PREFACE

I didn't start out to write a book. I am just an ordinary person with an extraordinary story to tell. And, the bigger the story grew, the more difficult it became to remember the details. I began to write them down on paper, like keeping a diary, mainly so I wouldn't forget things. As the *Fortuna*'s story evolved, I was urged to write a book so others could learn the story - that's how I became the author of this book, *Fortuna*.

It all started with a walk on the beach in 1970. Well, no. It actually started back in 1909 when the square-rigged sailing ship, *Fortuna*, left the port of Trapani, Sicily for a two year voyage to New York. Along the way, it encountered several terrible storms that challenged the strength of the ship and its crew. Both the *Fortuna* and her crew weathered the storms and continued on their charted course. After an unexpected stop in Barbados, the *Fortuna* weighed anchor and headed to New York.

On a stormy, foggy morning in January 1910, just twenty miles south of their final destination, the *Fortuna* was forced ashore in Ship Bottom by violent seas, becoming another fatal statistic in the Graveyard of the Atlantic off Long Beach Island, New Jersey. Although everyone was safely rescued from the ship, including a newborn baby, the ship was declared a total loss. The wreck reports filed by the lifesavers listed the conditions of the wreck and described the heroic operations performed at the time of the rescue. But, what I *really* wanted to know was, what happened to the family after they lost everything in that tragic shipwreck?

Let's go back to 1970 when I entered the picture. While I was walking on the beach on Long Beach Island, I picked up a little piece of red tile that had washed ashore and landed right at my feet. That piece of tile was the first of many pieces of the *Fortuna*'s puzzle. Things about the *Fortuna* continued to land at my feet. In 1983, the remains of the *Fortuna* which had been buried for seventy-three years resurfaced, along with an anchor the salvagers had left behind. I thought the anchor would make a wonderful monument for the town of Ship Bottom so I set out to recover it. And, while I was at it, why not try to find the "newborn baby" who was rescued from the shipwreck? My quest for information not only led me to the United Nations, the Smithsonian Institute, and the National Archives in Washington, DC, but took me across the globe to Sicily, looking for answers.

I knew that someday I would write a book about the *Fortuna,* and I knew that I couldn't write the story without knowing, firsthand, what it would be like to sail a big vessel like the *Fortuna.* Until then, my entire sailing experience included a few trips around the bay in a small Sunfish that always ended with me and the boat upside down in the water. When I learned that *Gazella,* the Tall Ship of Philadelphia, needed volunteers to do restoration work, I knew this could be my learning opportunity. I immediately volunteered as part of *Gazella's* restoration crew and worked there every weekend for an entire year. The first thing I learned was that when they called a "block party" it didn't mean a social gathering; it meant we were repairing the blocks used to raise and lower the sails! The reward for all my hours of hard labor was to sail the route once charted by the *Bounty* (as in Mutiny on) but at the last minute we were declared unfit to sail and were grounded. Still determined to get my sea legs, I learned of a square-rigger in the Caribbean that was looking for several new crew members. For what I called a "working vacation," I sailed on board the *Belle Blonde* as a "new salt" to learn the ropes. Believe me when I say it is really scary to be one hundred and fifty feet above the deck, trusting only my feet to hold me on the yard as I furled the sail. I also learned, firsthand, that seasickness is no joke. With my new sailing experiences under my belt - more accurately called my climbing harness- I felt I could write a story about the *Fortuna* with better than a fair degree of accuracy.

Not only did the *Fortuna* afford me the opportunity to grow my sea legs, but it did a lot to boost my confidence as well. As interest in the *Fortuna* increased, I was asked to share my story with many local organizations. I was never one to enjoy public speaking; I used to cringe at the thought of speaking in front of a large crowd. But not anymore. The *Fortuna* gave me the confidence I needed to tell my story no matter how large the audience, because now I knew more about the subject than they did.

Fortuna is a true story; the people and their stories are real. Little documentation of events leading up to the actual disaster exists, but from stories told to me by the only survivor of the wreck still living, along with the recollections of others who shared those times, I have tried to piece together a faithful portrayal of certain incidents as they might have occurred. Through personal interviews with people involved, the story comes to life on the pages of *Fortuna*.

Fortuna is a story that needed to be told. Though the circumstances under which we came to know the *Fortuna* and its owners were tragic, all the writings were not completely accurate. There were some events that started out as rumors and later recorded as fact. I felt compelled- that I owed it to surviving members of the family - to correct those errors and present the story the way it really happened.

Chapters

FORTUNA

The real value of a found treasure is determined by the minds of those who find it.

Summer - 1970

I don't know why I picked it up. It was not particularly pretty. But there was something about it that screamed "pick me up and take me home." I was drawn to it the way a piece of metal is drawn to a magnet. Perhaps it was its bright reddish color, a sharp contrast to the natural colors of the shells and pebbles on the white sandy beach of Long Beach Island. It wasn't very large; only about four inches square and half an inch thick. The edges were irregularly-shaped, worn smooth by the tumbling of the surf. It reminded me of a brick, worn thin by its time spent in the water. Upon closer inspection I could see some letters engraved on one side, and some lines and several points of a star on the other. Was there any value to this object? A walk along this section of the New Jersey shore that I call "my beach" can sometimes yield a treasure of great value; something determined by the minds of those who find it. I wondered if this newly found treasure had an interesting history, maybe going back hundreds of years. I placed the flat red brick-like object in my pail along with our other finds of the day and headed back home to our beach house.

Although my husband Greg had spent the summers of his childhood at the family homestead in Brant Beach, I was a newcomer to Long Beach Island. Several years after our marriage in 1964 we built our own summer home, also in Brant Beach. As summer residents, we anxiously looked forward to June when school let out and we packed up our gear and headed to the beach for the whole summer. Visions of carefree days just lying on the beach basking in the summer's sun filled our dreams. What a life! Those were the days before much thought was given to limiting one's exposure to UV rays. But the lazy days of summer idea didn't last long. After a week the thought of lying on the beach all day lost its appeal. With daughter Alison in hand, we decided to walk the beach to look for treasures.

Alison has always been extremely active and inquisitive. As a young child, it was a real challenge to keep pace with her energy level. Her body and mind were always racing ahead to the next moment. And her imagination? The simplest things could keep her busy for hours as she would lose herself in her own world of fantasy. Alison spotted them first, glistening in the sand as the bright mid-day sun made them sparkle like priceless gems in a jewelry store display case. She raced ahead to pick up one of the bright green emeralds before the outgoing surf could carry it back into the sea. At the innocent age of three, she was thrilled with her find. I agreed that, indeed, it was the prettiest emerald I had ever seen, silently thanking the litterbug who had carelessly thrown the Heineken bottle into the sea. Adults know these pieces of tumbled glass as sea glass. But to the young and the young at heart, they are truly gems of the sea. As we continued our walk along the beach, Alison gathered more diamonds, topazes and sapphires that had washed ashore. We also collected some shells, seaweed and colorful polished stones. And I even found another piece of the mysterious red brick-like object before we headed home. We oohed and ahhed and admired our treasures before placing them in a basket on the kitchen table. They were soon forgotten as other daily activities filled our lives.

Several days after our treasure hunt on the beach, a dear friend of the family we lovingly called Aunt Lydie came to visit. Although Aunt Lydie grew up and still lived in Manahawkin, on the mainland just seven miles over the Causeway, she had many Island friends whom she visited regularly. We considered ourselves very lucky to be counted among them. We served her homemade lemonade and freshly baked cookies at the kitchen table and complained about how hot the summer was, and that it was still only June. Aunt Lydie then noticed the red brick-like object in the basket on the table.

"Do you know what you have there?" she asked, knowing all the while that I probably did not.

"You mean this red brick with the lines and letters on it? I found it last week while walking on the beach. I thought it was interesting, but I don't know anything about it," I admitted. I could tell she was holding back, like a child with a secret needing to be told. "You know something about it, don't you?"

Lydie Neuendorf

French tiles carried as ballast on Fortuna

"Yes, I know where it came from. It came from the ship, *Fortuna*," she stated with a great deal of authority. "It wrecked up there in Ship Bottom. I think it was at 16th Street. I was only fifteen years old then, but I remember the day it wrecked."

Lydie Neuendorf was eighty-eight years old in 1983 when she shared some of the details of her life with me:

As soon as I could talk, my mother taught me to say, 'I was born Eliza Jane in Manahawkin on Bolton Lane, in 1895, Thursday afternoon at 5 o'clock, the 21st day of August.' As a child, I grew up in Manahawkin with my parents and grandparents. We visited Long Beach Island many times, going there by boat of course, for there was no bridge back then. I can remember all the excitement when the news reached us about a big sailing ship that got stranded and wrecked on the beach in Ship Bottom, and we were all anxious to see it. My Aunt Angeline's husband took us across the bay in his garvey, and we walked from the bay, across the island to the beach, and there it was. It was a big ship, lying on its side at the water's edge, still rigged for sailing. We spent most of the day climbing on the ropes. The hatch covers were missing from the deck so we could even get inside the hold. I still remember the curved ribs of the inside. Funny what makes an impression when you're young. I recall being inside it so well.

During the summer following the wreck [1910] I went back to the beach with my family, this time by train, for a Sunday School picnic. We had it at the site of the Fortuna *wreck. I remember that very well, too, because we had my baby brother with us. He was born in December of 1909 and was eight months old, and we all sat under the keel of the boat to keep him out of the sun. It was July, you know, and it was hot! The ship remained on the beach pretty much the way it was when it was wrecked. Most of it was still there in 1915 when I married. Oh, people took off souvenirs from here and there, you know, but for the most part, it was whole when the salvage crew came to cut it up.*

That was about the same time they began to build the new bridge. Remember the old drawbridge? Well, the first bridge was built in 1912; that was a swing bridge. I had a beau then and he had an old Maxwell car. The road was not built to the bridge yet. The bridge stood there, but it was not connected to the road. The men made a ramp from boards and pushed the car onto the bridge and we drove across. There was no road on the other side either, so we just turned around and came back. No car had

*ever crossed the bridge before. Charles Parker and I were the first people to
ride from Manahawkin to Long Beach Island.*

*When they built the new bridge in 1914, they took the little pieces of
metal like slugs made of iron or lead, which was the ballast from the ship
[Fortuna]. This was used for the counterweight of the new drawbridge.
They didn't waste anything in those days. The salvagers had to take the big
pieces of the* Fortuna *away on scows by way of the ocean. They took most of
it away, but there are still pieces on the beach, you know. There was always
something coming up. We often found pieces of tiles from the boat. Only
red ones. They washed out of the ship all over the beach. Oh yes, there were
lots of whole ones, too. We used to bring them home and use them in the
kitchen as trivets by the stove. I wish I had kept some, but that was such a
long time ago. After I was married in 1915, we lived at 23rd Street in Ship
Bottom. Looking north, there were only about a dozen little houses along
the railroad. I could count them on my hands. That's all there were. And
the dunes, why they were as high as the houses!*

And still, after all these years, pieces of those red tiles wash up onto
the beaches of Long Beach Island to the south of Ship Bottom. I was
ecstatic when I learned that my little piece of tile was linked to a bigger
piece of history. And I had the strongest feeling that this was only the
beginning. While the emeralds we gathered that day were truly great
treasures for Alison, I could feel deep within my bones that the little
piece of red tile would lead me on an adventure of a lifetime.

Summer/Fall - 1982

As the summers passed, walks on the beach yielded even more tiles,
piquing my curiosity with each new discovery. And the pieces I found
were getting bigger. The bigger the pieces were, the more writing I could
read. By joining several tiles together like pieces of a jigsaw puzzle, I
could read the inscription as clearly as if it had been engraved yesterday:
"ARNAUD ETIENNE & Cie ST HENRY MARSEILLE."

"Looks like French to me," I said out loud, though no one was
around to either hear me or respond. So I answered myself, "Now I
know where to start looking for answers."

I had so many unanswered questions about the tiles and was more determined than ever to find out where they came from, what they were used for, and why they were on the *Fortuna*. For me, the next step was obvious. The French I studied in high school, many more years ago than I'd like to admit, could finally be put to a useful purpose. Oh, Miss Dixon would be so proud! It was in the days before the computer and Google (if you can even imagine a time like that) that I sat at my typewriter and composed my letter: (originally written in French)

December 1, 1982

Arnaud Etienne & Cie
St. Henry, Marseille France

Dear Sirs:

A long time ago, in 1909, an Italian ship *Fortuna*, sailed from Trapani, Sicily. The ship ran aground during a storm on Long Beach Island, New Jersey, USA (on the Atlantic Coast of America) and was destroyed by the surf.

The *Fortuna* carried a cargo of red tiles which have been washing up on our beach over the past few years. I have quite a collection of these tiles, and have also managed to obtain a photograph of the ship. After all these years (73) the markings on the pieces are still quite legible and by piecing several together, I have come up with the name of your company.

I am assuming this is the name of the company where these tiles were manufactured. Hoping that is correct, and that your company is still in business is the reason why I write to you. I would like some information about these tiles to complete the details about our treasures. Can you please try to help me?

1. Is this the name of the company that made the tiles?
2. Are they still being made?
3. What were these tiles used for?

If you can supply any information about these tiles, I would appreciate your correspondence. When we uncover the mysteries of where they came from and learn a bit more about them, if you are interested in a piece for "your collection," I will be happy to send one to you.

Thanking you for your cooperation in advance,
Carole Bradshaw

I mailed the letter, thinking that two weeks was a reasonable time to expect a response. It never occurred to me that they might not respond at all. Each day I waited and each day for months I was disappointed: no response from France. Our daily family activities distracted me, and I soon forgot about the letter that I had hoped would answer all my questions about the *Fortuna* and the red tiles from France.

At any time, a ship could be caught in a storm due to oversight, overconfidence, or just plain bad luck. But once an emergency strikes, the cause matters far less than the solution.

The Fortuna – 1906

The Adragna Family – 1916
Maria, Captain Giovan Adragna
Antonina, Giuseppe, Anna, Saveria

January - 1909

The crew struggled for days against the powerful strength of the violent squall that continuously pelted them with snow and sleet. As the men braced themselves, another gust of wind sprang up and sent the ship reeling in all directions. Gathering all the strength they had left after battling the storm for better than half the four-hour watch, the best efforts of the captain and helmsman could not keep the *Fortuna* on course. A huge wave flooded the deck and flung the helmsman against the rigging as the *Fortuna* turned broadside and nearly capsized. The exhausted captain recovered his grip and struggled to bring the *Fortuna* back onto her course and hold her there as the next swell rolled beneath her bow. The unyielding storm continued to pound the *Fortuna*. The sky darkened as dusk approached, and the waves and winds that once sounded so far off were suddenly crashing down upon them. Less than thirty seconds elapsed since the last wave struck. Again, the sea swamped the *Fortuna*, sweeping tons of icy cold water the entire length of the deck. Inside, the noise of the sea pounding against the ship's steel hull was deafening. The weight of the rushing water crushed the skylight and water poured below, flooding the cabin. Captain Adragna descended the stairs and found his charts and papers floating in knee deep water. He ordered the cabin to be bailed out, and a temporary closure was made from an unused sail to cover the broken light. Little else could be done until the weather improved. In treacherous conditions such as these, only the most experienced seamen can react in time to save their ship from being caught up in the violent swells that would leave them to the mercy of the sea.

*   *   *   *   *

Giovan Battista Adragna, captain of the bark *Fortuna*, was forty two years old when he set sail for Marseille, and as a result of a recent medical examination, knew himself to be in good health. Taller than average height, standing several inches over six feet, he was an impressive man. His shoulders were broad, and his full moustache matched the dark color of his hair. Square jawed and confident, his face retained a healthy youthfulness. His weight of 185 pounds was a slight increase in what he weighed when he graduated from Umberto University in Naples, Italy at the age of twenty seven. He was not the wealthiest sea captain in the Sicilian port of Trapani, by any means, but he commanded great respect and admiration by his fellow seamen, and was idolized by every young boy who ever dreamed of someday filling his shoes. Always certain of what he wanted in life, Giovan had in large measure obtained it. Cautious by nature, particularly in matters of the heart, he proposed marriage only once. On his left hand, the stronger hand by his own choice, he wore a plain gold band, a symbol a decade old, of his marriage to Maria Savona, thirteen years his junior.

The third son of Giuseppe, a seasoned sea captain in his own right, Giovan could not remember ever wanting to be anything besides a sailor. He'd had a passion for ships ever since that first time his father took him to the Port of Trapani to show him his ship. When not out to sea, which was not very often, his father would take Giovan aboard his ship where they would sit on the deck and listen to the sailors swap tales - some taller than others - of their adventures on the open seas. It was not her young son's exposure to the harsh lifestyle of the sailors that frightened Maria the most; it was knowing that Giovan could easily fall from the dock into the water and drown. Rather than put an end to the precious hours spent with his son, Giuseppe did the most practical thing a father could do: he taught his son how to swim.

At the same time, thousands of miles across the globe in the small bay town of Manahawkin off the coast of southern New Jersey, a young boy named Isaac Truex, about the same age as Giovan, followed his father around like the proverbial shadow. They went everywhere together, spending hours upon hours on the banks of Barnegat Bay fishing; just the two of them most of the time. Occasionally, they would be joined by other locals wanting to catch up on the latest gossip. Or they would go deep into the marshy swamp where Isaac would run anxiously through the tall salt grass in search of a turtle to take home for a pet. And, just before heading home, Isaac would always be sure to gather a huge armful of the largest pinkest most fragrant rose mallows he could find as a peace offering to his mother for being late for supper, again. But what Isaac enjoyed most was going to work with his father at the Lifesaving Station in Ship Bottom. He would often launch their wooden surf boat into the ocean and pretend to be the captain of a sailing vessel caught in a violent storm, threatening to wreck on the dangerous shoals of the New Jersey shore. He would then envision a brave rescue at sea with all aboard being saved, of course. Isaac loved everything there was about the sea and learned at a very early age to respect her unpredictable moods. His mother never worried about his safety when playing around the water because at a very early age Isaac's father had taught him to swim.

Isaac and Giovan both loved the ocean with a deep passion. As they grew older, each pursued his career in a different direction. Although they lived thousands of miles apart, the very same ocean that separated them would one day bring them together.

Giovan Adragna graduated from Umberto University with a Universal License that enabled him to master ships in all the seas of the world. Life was wonderful for Giovan. He had already realized one of his two lifelong dreams: one was to be "Capitano" of a ship; the other was to raise a family. I've heard it said many times: when looking for a mate, a daughter will seek out the same characteristics as those of her father. And that was exactly why Maria Savona fell in love with Giovan Adragna almost at first sight. He was tall and handsome, strong yet gentle, and, like her father, was a man of the sea. Maria had grown up in a family of seafaring men. She watched her mother suffer through months of separation from her father, and she knew of the dangers he faced every day. This was a tough life for both the men who went to sea and the families they left behind. Yet it was the only life they knew and they accepted it without complaint.

Giovan was an aspiring captain taking on jobs from several prosperous companies in Trapani, Sicily. Although he spent long months at a time at sea, he treasured most the times when he was back at home with his family. By this time, Giovan and Maria had two young children, both girls. Antonina, born in 1903 and later Anna, in 1907 were the joys of his life. Being separated from his family was often unbearable.

As Giovan began to prosper, he hoped to realize his second dream: to own his own ship. When he spotted the ship for sale, he knew it was the one for him. It was a bark, an updated version of a clipper ship, built in 1869 at Rhiersteig-Schiffwerfte in Hamburg, Germany. That the ship was "built to last" was implied by the careful selection of materials and meticulous craftsmanship of its German shipbuilders. They were masters of their craft who believed themselves to be second to none. The ship had three masts with square sails on the fore and mainmast, and fore and aft sails on the mizzen (the rear mast). This configuration allowed for increased speed, and also reduced the number of crew required to sail. The hull was made of steel, a construction change employed towards the end of the nineteenth century. The ship measured 193 feet, 6 inches long by 33 feet wide by 20 feet, 9 inches deep and had a net capacity of 924 tons. (A ship's tonnage is measured as the volume of cargo that can be carried in the hold; it is not a measurement of weight.) The sails were in good condition, and the rigging needed only minor repairs. Two lifeboats still hung in their davits where they would hopefully remain until the ship was broken up after a long life of service. Yes, this was the ship he would purchase in partnership with Captain Baldassare Savona, his brother-in-law, and Aloisio Salvatore, father-in-law of Baldassare. Together they would name their ship *Fortuna*, meaning "good fortune" in Italian.

*   *   *   *   *

Giovan had just returned from a year's long journey and would be in Trapani only a month before he headed off to France on the *Fortuna* to begin a two-year voyage to New York. While docked in Trapani, the necessary repairs were made on the *Fortuna*. They also took on several new crew members. It is an accepted belief that no ship was better than the crew she carried. Giovan chose his crew with great care knowing they could make the difference between survival or death. His first mate, Michele Barbera, was a fine choice. Perhaps he was chosen for his appearance, a very fine looking man, much like Giovan himself when he first started as an apprentice. He was rather tall and youthfully slim, in his early to mid-twenties, though trying to look a bit older, he allowed his moustache to grow. As a mate, he was very capable and Giovan was confident with his choice.

The first mate was responsible for the cargo, supervising the loading and unloading at port. He also had to possess a knowledge of navigation, how to determine the ship's position with the aid of a sextant and a chronometer, and know a bit about seamanship so he could take over should the captain become incapacitated. The first mate usually climbed directly up the ladder to become a captain. This, too, was the dream of Barbera. The selection of the remaining twelve men was made from the seamen available at the time. There was always a supply of well-seasoned men ready and able to sail at a moment's notice. They, no doubt, had seen all kinds of weather and their years of experience were of great comfort to Giovan. They were all of Italian descent and most likely related to each other either through blood or marriage. There was a real feeling of camaraderie among the men and they worked well together as one.

The duties of the crew were divided into two watches, each under the command of either the captain or the first mate. Day and night, a seaman positioned at the helm was in charge of keeping the ship on a course set by the captain. In stormy conditions the strength of two men was often required to hold the wheel, all the while in danger of being swept overboard. A crew member was stationed at the bow to keep a lookout for signs of changes in the weather. In good weather the job was pleasant and undemanding, but it had to be done in rain, snow, sleet and scorching sun as well.

Watches were generally shifted every four hours, and while not on duty a sailor experienced few pleasures. Often he would try to catch a few hours sleep, still clad in his wet oilskins. Always wet, always ready. In fair weather before each new watch was called, the mate checked over the ship and assigned chores to the men as they began their shift. When the weather was good and all repairs had been made, there was always the endless duty of swabbing the deck to keep it free from mold which all too quickly grew upon its damp surface. When a gale struck and the call "all hands" was cried, the crew was rudely interrupted from work or rest, but responded with their usual dedication to duty. And so, day after day, week after week, month after month, their activities became routine, if not monotonous from their lack of variety.

After the crew had completed all the repairs, the *Fortuna* left the port of Trapani and headed to Marseille where they would dock and load the ship with ballast. It is not clear whether it was an oversight on the part of Captains Adragna and Savona, or a deliberate economic decision to sail without insurance on the *Fortuna* on this voyage. Whichever it was, it proved to be a costly mistake.

Back at home in Trapani, Maria was feeling the pain of the lonely years she spent while Giovan was away on his last voyage. She wanted no part of another two years without her husband. Taking her courage into her hands, she exercised her privilege as the master's wife to accompany him on this journey. She packed up the two girls and some personal belongings and headed to Marseille without a word of discussion with Giovan. She had never sailed on a voyage with him before, but she had made up her mind that this time she would - and that was all there was to it!

Giovan was not at all happy to see Maria and the girls when they showed up at the dock in Marseille. He was very surprised to see them because he and Maria had never discussed the idea of their going along on the voyage. He was angry that she had made such an important decision without consulting him first. Giovan knew all too well the dangers of taking his family on such a long ocean voyage. It would have been quite different had their route been within the Mediterranean, but this trip was across the open seas. Besides, his ship was not prepared for family living. It was a modest, hard-working cargo ship, geared for his basic needs and those of his crew. Although Giovan did his best to discourage his wife from joining him, she hit him in his weakest spot: his heart. Before long he was seen helping Maria and the children aboard the *Fortuna* with all their belongings.

The crew spent days getting the *Fortuna* ready for her ocean crossing, making sure that every inch of her was checked out and repaired before the word was given to weigh anchor. The loading of a sailing vessel was a fine art that was supervised by the first mate. Because the *Fortuna* would not be carrying any cargo, ballast had to be carefully calculated in order to keep the vessel steady. Everything had to be packed tightly to keep from shifting at sea. At the bottom of the hold went about fifty tons of kentledge - iron scraps from foundries of local industrial towns. Depending on the size of the ship, as much as one hundred additional tons of ballast was stowed above the kentledge. For ballast, the *Fortuna's* hold was loaded with roofing tiles manufactured by a local factory. Each red tile measured nine inches square and was marked with the name of its manufacturer, *Arnaud Etienne & Cie St. Henry Marseille.* Many bundles of tiles were strategically balanced in the hold until the proper weight was reached. Floor planking was then laid over the ballast. The last items placed on board were several animals, mostly pigs and goats, that would be slaughtered en route by the first mate as needed for food. The hatches were closed and sealed and the anchor cranked on board. Her topsails were loosened and she was escorted by a tug to the open sea, ready to begin the voyage.

It was January 6, 1909 when the *Fortuna* weighed anchor in Marseille and headed out to sea. This was going to be a long voyage, perhaps as long as two years. They were bound for New York charting a course by way of Montevideo, Uruguay. The *Fortuna* was a tramp cargo ship, meaning she hadn't been hired to carry cargo for a specific company; she would just sail from port to port looking for cargo to transport. As they took cargo on, they would sell off their ballast and hope to make a nice profit. Shortly after departure, Giovan turned the ship over to Barbera and went below to his cabin to record the first entry in his log book. He noted their time of departure, initialed the entry and closed the book. He unrolled his chart on the table in his crowded quarters and double checked the course he had set for the voyage. Yes, it would to be a long journey. He paused for a moment then rolled up the chart, extinguished the light and went to bed.

At the time they set sail the weather seemed rather mild for January, but as the weeks dragged on, the severity of the winter increased. The dangers hung over head like a black cloud. Just five weeks out of Marseille, the *Fortuna* was proceeding towards Montevideo before a howling squall of snow and sleet. The weather gave the ship a hard workout. The wood planking warped and the sails were weakened by salt water and mold. When anchored in the next port they would take care of the necessary repairs to make the *Fortuna* shipshape for the next leg of their journey.

Life at sea for Maria was very different than the life she was used to back home in Trapani where she lived so close to her extended family. Most of the time she was aboard the *Fortuna*, she was pretty much alone with the children. She really missed her family. Perhaps Maria had not thought her plan all the way through? But it was too late for her to second guess her decision. Besides, all that really mattered to her was that she was with her husband, and their family was all together. Maria knew this would be a dangerous voyage and that Giovan would have more to worry about with all of them on board. She shared with him her terrible fear that he would be swept up in a storm and that if he must die, then it would be her wish and the will of God that they all die together. The crew continued on their charted course with the skill and confidence of well seasoned mariners.

Giovan was delighted that Maria and the children were reasonably free from sea sickness on their first voyage. And though he would not readily admit it for fear of establishing a precedent, Giovan rather enjoyed having his family on board. He had the utmost confidence in his crew and first mate, and that left him precious time to spend with his family. He was very much a family man and felt as though he now had the best of both his worlds.

It was a well-accepted belief that a captain who had his family on board was more likely to take better care of his ship, though everyone already conceded that Giovan was about the best captain around. He was strict, though not tough; he had a way of making his crew feel completely confident in his abilities. They knew he meant business when it came to sailing the ship, yet he was compassionate in every other way. Giovan was like a teacher, sharing the responsibility of navigation with the members of his crew just so they could get the feel of the ship. But no matter how much authority he delegated to his mate and crew, in the end, he was responsible for judging how hard to push his ship. He carried the glory of being captain, a distinction that was well respected in the end of the 19th century, but the responsibility made him earn every penny of his salary.

Giovan's family did not intrude into the lives of those working aboard the ship. They mostly stayed below deck where it was a great deal safer for the children to be. Though Giovan did have misgivings at first, he did not resent his wife's intrusion into his world at sea. At the close of a tiring day, after fighting the angry sea for endless hours as he pushed to meet the demanding schedule he had set for himself, he drew a great deal of comfort from having his wife close by. He secretly wished she had joined him on his voyages sooner. Ah, what his men were missing.

Maria was intrigued by the life she lived while out at sea; she found it to be so peaceful. She marveled at the ship's speed as the wind silently propelled the ship along its course. There were no distractions; nothing but sky above and sea beneath as far as the eye could see. They rarely saw another vessel of any kind, yet she did not feel alone. In warm weather, she enjoyed sitting on the deck watching the sailors at work. Many of the crew had left families behind, or had long outgrown the "daddy role," and they enjoyed recapturing that part of their early years by playing with the girls. The children were a welcomed change of pace. Maria's days were always filled with activities centered on the care of her children. And still, her favorite moments were to sit on the deck with Giovan on a pleasant evening and watch the ever-changing skies, just talking about life and their family back home. She often referred to the *Fortuna* as her "home away from home."

As captain of the *Fortuna*, Giovan was well aware of the efforts required to keep his ship out of danger, and he had the greatest degree of confidence in the abilities of his crew. He knew they were the best there was, and knew he could not do better himself. He could comfortably leave the care of his ship to the crew and turn his attention to the health of his wife. At first Maria seemed to adjust quite well to the pitching of the boat as it sailed in the rough open waters. But she was beginning to experience a great deal of sea sickness even when the seas were relatively calm. Giovan was concerned. Perhaps so much time spent at sea had been too much for her. Maybe he had been selfish to allow her to be with him for this long journey. Still, he was worried since medical care was so far out of their reach. His fears for her health were soon allayed when they determined that it was not the sea that had caused her sickness. She was pregnant, and along with that came the all too familiar nausea of "morning sickness." In his mind, Giovan silently calculated the months of the trip still ahead of them and made a mental note to change his course. They would not make it to New York before the baby was born.

It felt like a breath of fresh air when the *Fortuna* reached the harbor in Montevideo in Uruguay. It felt good to be in calmer waters again. The Port of Montevideo was a usual stop-over for the *Fortuna*. During several previous dockings at the port, Giovan had established many friendships there. This time he would be especially proud to show off his wife and children to the many other captains who would be envious that he had brought them along. Maria was beginning to feel better, but with her increased size, tired more quickly. Instead of participating in playtime with her children, she was often seen just sitting on deck, watching. While in port, the crew continued to make the necessary repairs on the ship; there were sails to repair, and several of the lines also needed fixing. It was better to fix these things in the safety of the harbor than to wait until necessity forced the crew to fix them while under way.

Most of the crew had never been to New York, and the closer they got the more excited they grew. Other sailors had told them how exciting it was to sail into the Hudson River, and they were anxious to experience the thrill for themselves. Once all the necessary repairs to the vessel had been completed, there was little reason for them to remain. The crew pulled anchor and left Montevideo on September 6, 1909.

The *Fortuna* continued to travel to New York on the course set by Giovan. The weather had been favorable and they were sailing at a comfortable speed. But, just as Giovan had thought; New York was too far away. He studied his chart and calculated the distance to the nearest port: the *Fortuna* would dock in Barbados to wait for the birth of the baby.

Upon his arrival in Barbados, Giovan arranged with the harbormaster for a mid-wife to come aboard the ship when the time was ready. So they waited. While in port, the crew enjoyed the relaxation, the scenery and the good times. They continued to repair the lines and mend the sails, where needed, to keep their ship in top condition for the rest of their voyage. The more repairs they did now, the less work they would have to do in New York.

On the morning of November 25, 1909, Giovan notified the harbormaster that the time had come to quickly send the mid-wife to help deliver the baby. The harbormaster wished the captain good luck with the delivery, offering the hope that this time he would be blessed with a son. He asked that when his son was born, would he raise the flags on his ship so they could all come and welcome him. Giovan assured him that he would. A few hours passed before the mid-wife delivered a healthy baby girl to Captain and Mrs. Adragna. Giovan immediately ordered his crew to raise all the flags on the ship to announce the birth of the baby. When the townspeople saw the flags flying on the *Fortuna* they were jubilant. Now the captain finally had a son to carry on his family name. The people of the town ran to the *Fortuna* to see the captain's new son, but when they learned it was a baby girl, they were confused. Why did they raise all the flags? The flags were supposed to signal the arrival of a son, not another daughter. Giovan responded with great delight, "I have two other daughters who I never saw being born. When I saw this one being born, I figured it was worth raising the flags for her." Their healthy baby girl, Saveria Fortunata Marina (named after Giovan's sister, the *Fortuna* and her father's love of the sea), entered the world in the early afternoon of November 25, 1909 on the island of Barbados in The Netherland Antilles. Though not a son, Giovan could not have been more proud. It was a thrilling event in his life to actually see his child being born. With this blessed event behind them they could make plans for the last leg of their journey. On December 25, Christmas Day, 1909, the *Fortuna* weighed anchor once again and left Barbados heading towards the east coast of the United States to the Port of New York.

January - 1910

Just a few minutes before eight o'clock on the evening of January 17, 1910, Giovan turned the wheel over to his first mate, Barbera. Giovan was tired, feeling the toll of the long day, and was relieved that his watch was over. He retired to his cabin below and found Maria asleep, exhausted from a day filled with the endless duties of motherhood. He undressed, removing his oilskins which reeked of fresh linseed, then slipped beneath the covers beside his wife. Maria stirred and moved closer to Giovan. He apologized for awakening her and kissed her tenderly, treasuring this rare moment they shared alone together. He extinguished the light and the cabin remained dark until the next shift.

Giovan was awakened by the sound of a sudden storm that struck the *Fortuna* in the middle of the night. He quickly dressed and joined the crew on deck as they gathered to begin their midnight watch. The six exhausted crewmen went below and fell into their bunks, still dressed in their wet oilskins, ready to respond to the call of duty at a moment's notice. The remaining six partially rested crew joined Giovan and his mate on the deck and took over running the ship. Howling winds continued to pound the *Fortuna*. Strong winds whistled through the rigging and, catching in her sails, threw the ship in all directions at once. The wind and sea had grown so violent that holding a course was too dangerous and exhausting. It was time to stop fighting the elements and trim the ship so it would take care of itself.

The "all hands on deck" cry went out, rudely awakening the six weary men who longed for a few hours of much needed sleep. They staggered topside to join the others. They quickly climbed the rigging in total darkness, trusting the feel of their feet to keep them on the yard as they fought against the strength of the wind to furl each sail. Even in moderate weather, furling and unfurling the sails had to be done over and over again. As the wind changes, the amount of canvas a ship can safely carry would also change. A captain would always try to keep as much sail set as possible. He would shorten when the weather got worse, and put out more canvas when the weather improved. Very often the crew would spend the entire day struggling to take in all the sails only to be told later in the night that the storm was diminishing and be ordered aloft to break out every sail the ship could carry.

But this storm did not diminish. It continued to increase throughout the night. The *Fortuna* had shown that she could safely run before the biggest waves and the strongest winds, and she could survive sail-blasting squalls of snow and sleet. But could she weather this storm that was holding her so tightly in its grip? Despite the frigid sheets of rain, the men worked throughout the night furling all her sails until she met the storm head on with only her bare poles.

The dangerous shoals off the coast of New Jersey were well-known and feared by every captain of a ship. Many ships and lives have been claimed by these dangerous waters, which, for good reason, have been nicknamed "The Graveyard of the Atlantic." Charts proved useless; continuously shifting sands made them obsolete the minute they were printed. As the daylight hours turned into darkness, the weather took a turn for the worse, forcing the *Fortuna* to sail blindly through the dense fog. Giovan anxiously paced the deck, feeling very uneasy about this night. The seas were wild and the wind was strong. There was no moon to guide them through the thickening fog. They desperately needed to fix their position. Giovan feared they were getting into shallow waters and gave the order to the leadsman to take a sounding. Taking his position first on the port side, he threw out the heavy weight until it hit bottom. Then, blindly counting the knots in the dark with his frozen fingers, he reeled in the line. Mentally, he calculated the depth of the water beneath the ship's keel: one knot, six fathoms; two knots, twelve fathoms; and so forth. He quickly repeated the procedure on the starboard side. Anxious to finish the task, he then cautiously worked his way over the slippery deck to report his findings to the captain. Had the line really touched the bottom, or was it only a tug on the line that he felt when the ship took that sudden pitch? He was not sure. But, he reasoned: the reading was close enough. 1

Disaster at sea can happen without warning, or it can come after long days of dreaded anticipation. As the *Fortuna* pitched in the turbulent sea and water washed over the deck, Giovan clung tightly to a lifeline that stretched the length of the ship. For just a brief moment he turned his attention from the angry sea to consider the plight of his ship. He knew that the lives of all on board were in his hands. His thoughts were interrupted by the desperate screams of the lookout: "BREAKERS AHEAD."

All the experience in the world could not reverse their position. There was little time for anything more than a quick prayer. Giovan devoutly offered one to the Madonna of Trapani, the Patron Saint of Italian Sailors, but he was doubtful she would have time to respond. He braced himself against the rail and waited for the deafening sound of his ship being split apart by the shoals beneath the water. But there was only the sound of silence; the sound he anticipated did not come. Instead, the ship continued on an even keel, silently gliding closer and closer to the shore, her near empty hull barely clearing the sandbar. She stopped with a jarring thud on the sandy bottom of the ocean at 16th Street in Ship Bottom, New Jersey. Giovan stole a brief moment in the darkness of the stormy night to thank the Madonna of Trapani for answering his hurried prayer. The *Fortuna* stood upright, stuck in the sand as the turbulent surf continued to pound her hull. She was safe, for now, but far from being out of danger.

To abandon ship was to admit defeat. As captain of the ship, it was up to him to decide the right moment to leave the ship and seek safety ashore. Giovan turned his head to focus his eyes on the lifeboats that had been placed on the ship when she was built forty-one years earlier. They still hung in the davits, neatly covered with canvas, waiting to be used in case of an emergency. Was it time to launch them, he wondered? Thoughts of launching a lifeboat in the turbulent surf and guiding it through the towering breakers raced through his mind. But he knew his sailors' lives were on the open sea. His men had no knowledge of these waters or the beach beyond the breakers. And he, himself, knew of sailors who had lost their lives while trying to save themselves from a stranded vessel. He should wait and hope they had been spotted from the shore and could be rescued by the surfmen who could do the job best. No, he would not launch the lifeboats; not yet.

The regulations say you have to go out, but they don't say you have to come back.

Motto of the U.S. Life Saving Service

January - 1910

The men at the station had watched the storm build all day and expected it to get much worse before it got any better. As the surfmen gathered inside the sanctuary of Ship Bottom Lifesaving Station No. 20, their thoughts and conversations wandered back to the memorable rescue of those aboard the *Abiel Abbott* seven years before, almost to the day.

June 1904

Surfman C.V. Conklin,
Ship Bottom Life Saving Station
Manahawkin, New Jersey

Sir:-
Transmitted herewith is a gold life-saving medal of honor awarded to you under the provisions of Acts of Congress approved June 20, 1874, and May 4, 1882, in recognition of your heroic conduct on the occasion of the rescue by you and your comrades of five men from the wreck of the barkentine, *"Abiel Abbott,"* under the following circumstances, as shown by the testimony of eyewitnesses:
On the 20th of January, 1903, the *Abbott*, while on her way from Turks Island, W.I., to New York City, heavily laden and drawing 17 feet of water, went aground on the outer edge of the Ship Bottom Bar, coast of New Jersey, at about 8:15 o'clock in the evening. As soon as she stranded she showed a signal of distress which was answered by Patrolman B.P. Pharo of your station, who burned his Coston signal in promise of

assistance if possible. Pharo then made his way as fast as he could to the station, where he arrived about 9 o'clock, the weather having constantly increased in severity. The night was intensely dark, the wind and sea were very high, and a heavy rain storm had set in.

Immediately upon receiving from Pharo information of the disaster, Keeper Truex telephoned to Keeper Falkinburg of the Harvey Cedars Station on the north, and to Keeper Mathis of the Long Beach Station on the south, requesting their aid, and then with his crew hastened to the scene. As soon as he arrived the Lyle gun was placed in action, but the first projectile did not quite reach the wreck, as stated by those on board who heard the shot fall a little short in the water. A second projectile, however, landed on board, but nevertheless they could not avail themselves of it because it fell about amidships, while the sea was so rough as to confine all hands to the extreme after part of the vessel. The whole hull, save the quarter-deck, was submerged and the waves were rolling deeply over it. Two more shots were fired, but the wreck could be located only by the faint glimmer of a light in the rigging, which was scarcely perceptible, and whether the projectiles landed on board or not, the shipwrecked men were unable to leave the little area of comparative safety which still remained to them.

The night was now so dark that only the break of the waves close on the shore could be seen, and all the conditions were so adverse that no sane man would have attempted to launch a boat before daylight. So, the survivors testify, was their own opinion, although they devoutly prayed for assistance. Under these circumstances you and your comrades of the three crews now assembled were obliged to wait and fret inactive on the beach until there should be sufficient light to justify an attempt to push out into the heavy breakers among the dangerous masses of wreckage which already encumbered the water. Between 3 and 4 o'clock in the morning the mainmast fell, but hung alongside for an hour or more, when the fore and mizzen masts also gave way. With the fall of the mainmast one of the sailors madly jumped into the water and was never seen again. When the other masts went, the remaining eight men were dragged overboard, but by means of the tangled spars and rigging still attached to the wreck, five of them managed to struggle back to the top of the cabin. Three perished.

At the first sign of dawn, while you and your comrades were straining your eyes seaward, trying to pierce the fog, a faint outcry from the wreck was detected, and instantly all hands as one man, jumped for the boat. Five of your own crew and one from the Long Beach station grasped the pulling oars, while Keepers Truex and Mathis took places in the stern to handle the steering oar and direct the movements. Surfmen stood in the water on each side of the boat to keep the wreck stuff clear, and at an opportune moment succeeded in safely shoving her out without damage from the planks, timbers, and general debris, which were thrust about by the waves with deadly force. Mr. Jones, a wreck-master who was present, says that when the launch was made he thought the chances were ninety-nine in a hundred that the boat would be smashed. Nothing daunted, however, by dint of powerful work and skillful handling she reached the bar sufficiently near the wreck to make out the five men still on board, but although every effort was exhausted by the sturdy oarsmen, she could make no further headway and, battered and scarred, but fortunately still seaworthy, was obliged to return. The Captain of the *Abbott* states in his testimony that he was sure you could not reach the wreck.

The gun was again resorted to, but just as the second shot was being fired, the cabin top, to which the men were clinging, broke adrift and became involved in the great flood of wreckage from the *Abbott*, which was now swiftly going to pieces. Again you and your comrades leaped to the boat and shoved her off. Every man present was eager to have a part in the rescue, and in the rush two from the Long Beach station found places at the oars, while Keepers Truex and Mathis again stood in the stern at the steering oar. With consummate skill and faultless courage the boat was driven forward, happily without serious injury, until it reached the five almost exhausted sailors and took them in. A landing was soon safely effected, but not long after, Frank Laven, one of the rescued men, expired from an ugly wound in the temple.

"The launching of the surfboat", says the investigating officer, Lieutenant Bertholf, R.C.S., "twice that morning through the heavy surf, filled with timbers and all sorts of wreckage, bristling with nails and spikes and bolts, was a feat that the Ship Bottom crew and the Life-Saving Service have reason to be proud of." Captain Hawkins of the *Abbott* says, "I did not think it possible for them to get to us, but somehow they did, and got us ashore, and I think it is a miracle that I am alive to tell the tale. No men could have done more than the life-savers did." That every man who went in the boat on either occasion freely imperiled his life is apparent beyond question.

It affords me great pleasure to act as the medium for the award of the accompanying medal in testimony of so heroic an achievement, avouched by experienced surfmen amply capable of estimating its merits.

> Respectfully,
> L.M. Shaw   (Leslie M. Shaw)
> Department of Treasury
> Secretary
> June 1904   2

A gold medal was a real personal treasure to each man, one that they earned and truly deserved. But they unanimously agreed that one *Abiel Abbott* was enough and hoped for a peaceful, uneventful night.

Shipwrecks were an all too common occurrence along the coasts of the United States during the 18th and 19th centuries. As European trade increased, so did the number of shipwrecks. The man credited for establishing the United States Life Saving Service was William A. Newell. While visiting Long Beach Island in 1839, he was horrified as he helplessly watched a shipwreck take the lives of the captain and his crew just three hundred yards from the safety of the shore. When Newell was elected as a representative in Congress for the maritime region from Sandy Hook to Little Egg Harbor, New Jersey, the first thing he did was apply for federal funds to build lifesaving stations along the coast. An increase in the number of stations along the coast did reduce the number of deaths from shipwrecks, but the system was far from perfect. The surfmen who manned the equipment were volunteers, mostly local baymen who, more often than not, were unprepared to handle the dangers of a rescue.

Long Beach Island's first lifesaving station was built in Harvey Cedars in 1848. All U.S. Lifesaving Stations were built exactly the same. The shape and size of the building, both inside and out, were all alike. There was a large boatroom, a kitchen, two sleeping compartments and a storage room. All stations were painted the same buff color with dark green shutters. The stations were built facing eastward allowing a direct path to the beach from the boatroom where the self-bailing boat was already on a carriage ready to be put into action. Unlike in the beginning when the stations were staffed by volunteers, they were now manned by a paid crew. Their $40 monthly salary was standard for the time and was enough to attract dedicated men who did a good job under the most difficult circumstances. But little effort was made to practice launching the surfboat or learn how to use their equipment. Often, when required at the time of a wreck, their skills were terribly slow. It was evident that more training was needed to prepare these men to meet the challenges of their job. As the Life Saving Service became more organized, daily drills were held to train the men to work more effectively. The men would practice launching the surfboat over and over again until the eighty minutes they once took to rig the boat had been trimmed to a mere five minutes. Both the Keeper and his crew were chosen from a group of local fishermen who proved themselves to be capable surfmen. Their success and sometimes even their lives were often dependent upon the abilities of each other.

*   *   *   *   *

Lifesaver Horace Cranmer discovered the stranded Fortuna on January 18, 1910 while on patrol.

Upstairs in the cozy second floor quarters of Lifesaving Station No. 20, slept four of the six surfmen who lived at the station from November to April, a time known as "the wreck season." The two others were out on patrol and were due to return momentarily. Isaac Truex, Keeper of the station, dozed at his desk in the upstairs office. It was 1:45 a.m., Tuesday, January 18, 1910.

Surfman Horace Cranmer, a man in his early forties, dragged his lean, tired body out of the bunk that was a bit too short for his six foot plus frame. Still half asleep, he stumbled as he crossed the dark room and pushed open the door that led him down the stairs to the boatroom. The room felt icy cold and a chill shook his body. He grabbed a woolen blanket and wrapped it around himself before heading to the kitchen to put more wood on the dying fire. First he took a detour up the steep, spiraling stairs to the lookout tower so he could see what was in store before starting his patrol. He could not see through the icy mist frozen on the window. With the edge of his fingernail, he scraped the ice from a small section of glass. Peering through the window, he could see nothing through the glass, now opaque from the wind-driven sand of last season's storms. He cracked open the window to get a better view but could barely see through the heavy fog rolling in from the sea. Visibility was near zero. He could just about make out the two dark shadows coming up over the dunes through the fog. As the figures came closer, Horace was relieved to see that it was just surfmen Pharo and Conklin returning from their watch. "Some night this is going to be," he muttered under his frosty breath as he descended the stairs to the kitchen.

Just as Horace expected, the fire had almost died out. He selected several good-sized oak logs from the freshly stacked woodpile and tossed them on the fire. The station dog, Tippy - a friendly, dependable mixed breed - was asleep on the rug by the fire; she raised her head and heaved a tired sigh of appreciation. Horace patted her head in silent greeting as he passed by. He walked down the narrow, dimly lit hallway then opened the door to the large boatroom. On the far side of the room he found his locker, unlatched its door and began to dress for his watch. It was raw and cold, and he could almost feel the force of the strengthening wind as it curved around the corners of the station. Storm clothes were in order for this night, for sure. Horace decided to wear two heavy shirts buttoned all the way to his chin to keep out the cold air. Hurriedly, he tucked his thick woolen pants into his rubber boots, lifted his jacket from the hook at the back of the locker, and then shut the door. Tonight he would wear his dark blue pea jacket - not the regulation lifesaving jacket with his #1 patch on the left sleeve - just the plain, rugged storm coat which he often thought showed too many years of dedicated service.

Abram Salmons, nicknamed "Brad" by everyone who knew him, would be Horace's partner on this stormy night. They would patrol the two mile stretch of beach together. They were a well matched pair, Brad and Horace. Not because they were so alike, but because they were so different. What character traits Brad possessed, Horace lacked, and vice versa. Brad was well organized, calm and rational. Horace was a bit disjointed and impulsive. Brad was slow and methodical; Horace quick and undisciplined. Yet the two were a perfect pair. When called upon to handle an emergency, their different ways melted into a perfect blend of common sense.

Brad entered the boatroom more wide awake than Horace. Though a good fifteen years older than most of the men, he required a lot less sleep and always began his watch completely refreshed. He proceeded to dress in his quiet, efficient manner. His boots were, for practical purposes, several sizes too big to accommodate the extra pair of socks he would need on very cold nights - like tonight. But to him, they felt comfortably "broken in." Brad had almost finished lacing his boots when the two o'clock bell sounded. He pulled on his jacket, hat and gloves and then turned out the light.

As they walked in silence along the hallway to the main office, Horace struggled to button his jacket, pausing when he reached the spaces where two buttons were missing. He had hoped to replace them before now, but. . . well, maybe there would be more time tomorrow. He was already running late for his shift. As soon as they reached the office, Brad, who was dressed and ready to go, began to gather the equipment to take with them on their rounds. Horace continued to dress, tying a scarf around the opening where the buttons were missing, then searched for his hat. He did not choose the regulation blue cap with the words "U.S. Life Saving Service" emblazoned in white across the brim. Instead, he chose to wear the new blue one with white stripes that his wife, Minerva, knit him for Christmas. He pulled it down over his ears and covered it with the familiar So'wester to keep him dry. Fully dressed, both men were ready to begin their beat.

Conklin and Pharo returned from their patrol and as they entered the station, the wind caught the door, smashing it into the wall with a loud bang. Tippy awakened from her sound sleep and excitedly ran to greet the returning patrolmen. It was no secret that Tippy liked Conklin best, and those feelings were affectionately returned.

"Fierce storm out there," reported Conklin. "The weather's not fit for even a dog." Tippy disappeared, reclaiming her favored spot on the rug by the fire. The men exchanged a few brief words about the conditions outside then headed to the kitchen to warm themselves by the fire. In passing, Horace could not help but hear the snickers his dress received from Pharo. Sure, he looked more like an Eskimo about to brave the frigid temperature of an Alaskan night than a lifesaver about to patrol the coast of New Jersey. But tonight there seemed little difference between the two. Not tonight. It was extremely cold out there and he knew better than to skimp on warm clothing, no matter how peculiar he looked.

The men of the Lifesaving Stations were responsible for patrolling the coast of Long Beach Island, dividing the hours from sunset to sunrise into three watches. At the beginning of each watch, two men set out from the station patrolling their beats, one to the right, the other to the left, until they met the men from adjacent stations. In severe weather, the men would often patrol in pairs. The brass cheque bearing the surfman's number was exchanged as proof to the Keeper that they had performed their duty. The relieving watches were kept up until sunrise, and in bad weather, throughout the day.

Horace removed the brass cheque bearing his #1 and Brad the #5 from the board hanging in the corner by the door, then pushed hard against the wind to open the door. The wind fought against them but they pushed even harder and finally won the battle. A gust of icy, cold wind slapped them hard across their bare cheeks. It was not a friendly welcome. Suddenly a blast of wind caught the door and slammed it shut behind them, officially signaling the beginning of their watch. Together the two men walked out into the fog, heading north to begin their rounds.

Walking side by side in silence, Horace and Brad trudged through the driving snow and sleet as the sharp edges of blowing sand pierced their faces like sharp needles. They were often forced to walk backwards against the wind for a bit of relief. But still they continued, their eyes searching the distance for a ship in distress. They strained their eyes constantly looking for clues: a flicker of light, a faint outline of a ship just beyond the breakers, or an object from a ship that washed ashore. Looking. They were always looking. A lantern was the only visible sign of life on the dark beach. The fog was extremely thick; the light from their beacon barely able to penetrate it. The temperature felt much colder than the thirty degrees registered on the thermometer back at the station. The dreadful weather was slowing them down, taking them forever to go just a few feet. As the gusting winds whipped around them, Horace readjusted the scarf to close the vent in his jacket created by the missing buttons. How tempted might they have been to skip this watch? Who would miss just one patrol? They would. Each man took extreme pride in performing his duty without the slightest concern for himself. It's just the way they were. They could feel it in their bones: this was going to be a very long night.

They were only minutes into their shift when, not more than a distance of 300 yards off shore, they could see the unmistakable outline of a ship's hull through the thick, heavy fog. It was a sign their eyes were trained to recognize but hoped they would never see. Surfman Brad Salmons withdrew the gun he carried and, with careful aim, discharged a red flare to signal the distressed ship that help was on the way. Above the roar of the surf, he faintly heard the cries of the sailors aboard the stricken ship, gratefully acknowledging that they'd been discovered.

This troubled ship the lifesavers discovered in the early morning of January 18, 1910 was the bark, *Fortuna*. Whether by the skills of the crew or by divine intervention, the ship had been carried over the sandbar and through the roaring surf only to be left stranded on the beach. There she stood in constant danger as the violent surf threatened to undermine her keel and drop her on her side into the sea.

Horace quickly made a mental note of their position. There were no landmarks on the beach, just one rising sand dune after another, silhouetted behind a veil of thick, dark fog. But he knew this beach like the back of his hand and could fix his position with a good degree of accuracy, with or without landmarks. With no time to waste, the two men hurried back to the station. "Ship ashore! Ship ashore!" they yelled as they barged through the door of the station. Their noisy entrance was enough to awaken even the soundest of sleepers on the second floor loft. Though still half asleep, the men knew what the noise meant: it was time to prepare for a rescue. The surfmen threw open the doors of the boatroom and rolled the boat carriage down the ramp, ready to be put into service. All available hands were required to drag the heavy carriage through the wet sand, always in the worst possible weather. It would take them over an hour just to travel the short distance of one-half mile to the site of the stranded ship.

The Ship Bottom lifesavers, being the closest to the stranded ship, were the first to arrive on the scene at 4:35 a.m. A single, flickering lantern dimly illuminated the beach. Each man, well trained in his duties, proceeded to handle the apparatus assigned to him. They would first try to remove the people from the stranded ship by using the breeches buoy. If unsuccessful, they would resort to launching the surfboat.

The breeches buoy consists of a pair of short, loose canvas pants (breeches), suspended from a doughnut-shaped cork life preserver (buoy). The buoy is suspended by ropes from a pulley block which rides on a line stretched taut between the ship and the shore. The person to be saved would step into the breeches and the lifesavers on the shore would pull the buoy from ship to shore. It worked fairly well for rescuing men, but the breeches buoy was not all that well suited for transporting women and children.

Brad shot a line from his Lyle gun at twenty-foot elevation. It flew against the strong wind, but fell short of the wreck. The ship was further out than he thought. The line was hauled in and reloaded. Another shot was fired at twenty-four foot elevation, this time reaching the vessel. A sailor on the stranded ship hauled the whip line aboard, but a chain on the end of the yard fouled so the whip line would not work. Had they been able to secure the whip line, the lifesavers would have attempted rescue with the breeches buoy. However, their attempts had failed and further efforts were suspended. They would resort to launching the surfboat.

Now it was 5:00 a.m. After a long and tiring journey dragging their heavy equipment through the wet sand, the assisting crews from Harvey Cedars and Long Beach arrived at the rescue site. Come 6:00 a.m. the storm still showed no signs of weakening. There was no thought of waiting for calmer waters. The decision had been made. By the light of the early dawn, the surfmen launched the surfboat. Truex took his position at the steering oar, guiding the boat through the choppy breakers. The surfmen, in their rowing position with their backs to the dangerous sea, kept their eyes steadily fixed on their keeper, following his every direction as they skillfully maneuvered their small boat through the huge waves.

The first attempt to launch the surfboat was unsuccessful. The turbulent sea filled the boat with water and she capsized, tossing the surfmen into the frigid water. The weight of their water soaked clothing made it difficult for them to stay above water. Kept afloat by their lifebelts, they struggled to shore to right the boat for a second or, if necessary, even a third try.

On board the ship, the greatest concern to Giovan was the safety of his passengers. While he worried about his crew as though they were his own family, he knew they could handle this difficult situation. He was most concerned with the safety of his wife and children who lacked the experience to handle an emergency at sea.

Giovan descended the steps to the cabin to begin preparations for a rescue from the shore. He found the two older girls, Anna and Antonina, dressed in warm clothing and sitting on the floor in the center of the cabin where the ship appeared to be more stable. Extremely frightened by the possibility of sinking, Maria frantically built a nest of blankets and heavy clothing in the far corner of her quarters. She placed her tiny baby in a burlap sack and buried her deep within the pile, providing a soft cushion against the violent storm. Tucked securely within the bedding, baby Saveria was quickly rocked to sleep by the rolling motion of the doomed *Fortuna*.

On the beach, the lifesavers launched the surfboat into the turbulent surf and quickly disappeared behind a thick curtain of fog. As the remaining surfmen stood helplessly behind, thoughts of the Life Saving Service's motto filled their minds: *"The regulations say you have to go out, but they do not say you have to come back."*

The surfmen approached the *Fortuna*, carefully securing their boat to the unsteady vessel. Great care was needed to prevent their small boat from colliding with the huge hull of the stranded ship. Within minutes, the exhausted surfmen boarded the *Fortuna*, ready to perform a job they knew well: the rescue. Keeper Isaac Truex was the first to board. The passengers and crew were extremely frightened, yet they were reluctant to leave the ship. Truex quickly realized the crew did not speak English. He approached the captain and, as best he could under the circumstances, described the dangerous situation they were in and told him they were ready to begin the rescue. But Giovan did not understand the urgency. He knew his ship was in trouble, but it had not broken apart like he thought it would. He had faith that the rough sea and higher tide would later be in their favor and carry the ship back to deeper waters. No, he was not ready to be taken off his ship. He would wait it out on board.

The surf became more violent as another storm approached. Truex was concerned that the ship would not survive another battering in the surf. He tried to convince Giovan that it was time to leave the ship while it was still possible for the lifesavers to navigate through the surf, but the captain wanted no part of leaving his ship. He did, however, request that some messages be sent to their agent in New York, and Truex complied.

Truex was not at all pleased with Giovan's decision to remain on board the stranded vessel. Things were bad enough now and he knew they would get worse as the storm intensified. Admitting defeat, Truex headed his surfboat back to shore, leaving surfmen Austin and Horace on the *Fortuna* to clear the whip line and make it useful in case it was needed.

Back at the station, Truex contacted Merritt Chapman Wrecking Company and requested they send their rescue tug, *Relief,* to the site of the stranded vessel. It was thought, and hoped, that the tug could tow the ship into deeper waters where she could be set free. With the intensity of the storm continuing to build, it was a risky plan to even consider.

Truex returned to the *Fortuna* a few hours later at 10:45 a.m. High tide was approaching, making it more dangerous for the sailors to remain on board their ship. It was flood tide at 11:00 a.m. and the churning surf left little beach to perform the rescue mission. Violent waves were tossing the *Fortuna* in the turbulent surf like a bobbing cork. The high waves were beginning to move the vessel in a sideways direction, and the lifesavers feared the ship would be undercut by the waves and heel over on her side. The time had come to order - not request - the captain and his passengers to leave their doomed ship.

The Ship Bottom lifesaving crew launched their surfboat again. Guiding the small boat through the rolling breakers required all the skill the men possessed. To board a ship in the middle of a storm was a dangerous task. One false step and they could be tossed into the swells and drowned. With the skills they were trained to use, the surfmen secured their boat and climbed aboard the *Fortuna* to begin the rescue.

The lifesavers steadied the surfboat as it heaved against the tall breakers. Surfman Horace Cranmer lowered the two small girls into the boat, but Maria would not come. The more he tried to pull her into the boat, the more agitated she became, refusing to budge. Finally, he ordered her to "just get in the boat." Instead she turned and ran towards her cabin. Horace followed. Maria started to gather the pile of blankets from the corner to take with her in the boat. Horace was angered by the delay. The safety of the passengers and crew came first; personal possessions, second. Maria continued to put up such a fuss it became obvious she would not leave the ship without her pile of belongings. Rather than argue with her, Horace scooped up the pile and carelessly tossed it into the bottom of the surfboat before joining the others in their laborious row towards shore.

Safely ashore, Horace assisted Maria and young Anna out of the surfboat. Her other daughter, Antonina, was carefully handed to the outstretched arms of a crew member standing on the beach. Horace picked up the pile of blankets and tossed them on the dry sand well above the incoming tide and left to help secure the surfboat. Other members of the service were there to give aid and comfort to the stricken family. Although the language difference made it difficult to communicate at times, it was dwarfed by the compassion and care being offered to Long Beach Island's latest victims of disaster.

Horace walked over to grab a blanket or two from the pile on the beach to wrap around the children to keep them warm. He heard a strange noise coming from the pile and was surprised by what he found.

"Well, what do you know? Hey, guys! Come look what I found in this pile of blankets. It's a baby. Looks like a newborn one," Horace remarked as he gently removed the crying baby from the burlap sack. "It's a little wet but none the worse for wear." With his rough, weathered hands he tenderly tucked the baby between the two missing buttons on his jacket and pressed the cold baby against his warm body. Spotting the rescued family standing on the beach, he walked over and handed the baby to the worried mother. Horace stole a backward glance at the pile of blankets and muttered something under his breath that no one could quite make out, then readied the surfboat for another launch. As he pushed the surfboat away from the shore, he strained his eyes to catch a glimpse of the baby being caressed by its mother. No one noticed the tender smile that briefly crossed Horace's face just before he braced the boat against the strength of the roaring surf for another trip to the doomed vessel to rescue the remaining survivors.

The last rescue surfboat to leave the *Fortuna*, manned by Isaac Truex, carried Giovan Adragna who still showed reluctance to leave his beloved *Fortuna* behind. Both men silently thought back to their younger days when they dreamed of what they would do when they grew up. This tragic event had brought them together, each doing the job they were trained to do and the one they loved the most. Giovan wondered what would become of his ship. And, being a captain was the only occupation he had ever known. Now, at only forty-three, would all this come to an end? Isaac Truex remained proud that his years of experience and training had prepared him to safely rescue everyone from the battered *Fortuna*. Sadly, Captain Adragna turned his back to his ship and bid a silent farewell as Truex steered the surfboat towards the shore to reunite him with his family. The rescue operation was completed by 1:30 p.m. The report listed that all seventeen on board were safely rescued. It makes no mention of the courage and bravery shown by the lifesavers during this tragic event.

The day was cold; the thirty seven degree air chilled them to the bone. It was not the time for standing on the beach rehashing the disaster that had nearly cost them their lives. The work of the lifesaving crew did not end with the rescue. The Adragna family and crew were taken to the station where preparations were already being made for their housing. The neglected fire was rekindled and fresh coffee brewed, filling the room with a pleasant aroma. Wet and frozen garments of the rescued victims were exchanged for dry clothing in a variety of colors and sizes. Keeper Truex designated the least weary of his men to tend to the needs of the victims while the others retired to rest until it came time to relieve the watch.

The additional seventeen people made it a lot more crowded inside the small Ship Bottom Lifesaving Station, yet the daily routine continued. Unfortunately, a shipwreck was nothing new to the lifesavers. They had done it so many times before. But caring for young children, especially a newborn baby, was unfamiliar territory to them. Conversation was sparse among the lifesavers and the *Fortuna's* Italian crew because, try as each might, they could not understand one another. The baby was the only one who spoke a common language: a newborn's cries are the same in any language. Young Anna and Antonina especially enjoyed playing with the station's dog, Tippy. All this new activity released the warm and caring feelings the lifesavers had forgotten they had while they spent the lonely winters on Long Beach Island. Word of the new "guests" quickly spread throughout the Island, and many of the local women offered their homes to the new mother and her children. Many a resident of Ship Bottom claimed to have rocked the baby to sleep to the tune of a familiar American lullaby. While the crew and Maria and the girls were often seen helping out around the station, Giovan was nowhere in sight; he was busy elsewhere making arrangements for their return to Trapani. There were no other rescues during the eight days the *Fortuna* victims were housed at the station.

For days the storm continued to loosen the *Fortuna* from her perch, tossing her into the swirling sea, turning her broadside to the ocean. Waves continued to batter against her keel, forcing her to list badly to her port side. On January 22, 1910 at 3:00 p.m., the *Fortuna* fell over onto her side. The sea washed over and around her hull, sinking her still deeper into the sand. All hopes for sailing the *Fortuna* again had vanished. She could never be righted; she could not be saved. The *Fortuna* had become another casualty off the coast of Long Beach Island, New Jersey. It was an incredible achievement, by any standards, that all lives were saved; except, perhaps, by the lifesavers' own.

The *Fortuna* lay abandoned on the beach only a few blocks from the lifesaving station where the family was being housed, yet they did not return to see her. What was there to see? She was no longer a majestic ship. Her towering masts were now split and dangling in the surf as the icy water washed over her fallen body. No, she was not a pretty sight. It was best to remember her as she was, a proud ship ready to meet the demands of the seas she had once called home.

But others not so fondly tied to the *Fortuna's* past came from all over the Island and the mainland to see this once gallant ship which would no longer sail. Souvenir hunters removed whatever pieces of the ship they could cart away, not with any thought of monetary gain, but merely to serve as a reminder of this tragic event. The pieces of red roofing tile the *Fortuna* had carried as ballast from Marseille were scattered on the beach like calling cards, just waiting to be collected by passersby. As required by law, the Life Saving Service provided armed guards to keep watch over the wreck until the final disposition could be made by its owners.

Giovan could not stay away and secretly returned to the beach one more time, his gaze fixed at the pitiful sight of his doomed ship. His face betrayed feelings of both despair and relief. Everything above deck had been smashed, yet the sea had claimed few of their personal items that had been stowed inside the cabin. Everyone on board had been saved, including several animals that were trapped inside the hull. His ship was a total loss, but they owed their lives to the men of The U.S. Life Saving Service.

Before leaving the site of the beached *Fortuna*, Giovan took one last look around and caught a glimpse of the ship's log floating in the turbulent surf. He waded towards it, but as he stretched to grab it, a wave came and swept the book out of reach. And with this, the final chapter of the *Fortuna* came to a close. The voyage was over. They had run aground on an island they knew nothing about, in a place where strangers had become friends. They were all alive, and for that, he was thankful. There was no time to waste feeling sorry for oneself. Giovan knew of the many challenges that lie ahead, and as master of the ship and head of his household, he took the heavy burden squarely upon his own shoulders.

The fate of the *Fortuna* left little for the imagination. She could not be left on the beach, stranded like a beached whale. While the family was housed at the lifesaving station in Ship Bottom, Giovan negotiated with a salvaging company in Tuckerton to remove the ship from the beach. The total value of the ship was listed at $8,000. The loss to the Adragna family was even greater. It was a financial disaster for the family since there was no insurance on the *Fortuna* at the time of the wreck. The family had lost their home, and Giovan had lost his livelihood. For a captain to lose his ship is a real disgrace, no matter what the circumstance. Some even thought disgrace was worse than death. The word on the beach, and later printed in the local newspapers, was that Captain Giovan Battista Adragna, the forty-three year old captain of the gallant bark, *Fortuna*, had committed suicide while grieving over the loss of his ship and the cancellation of his command.

Only eight days after the *Fortuna* wrecked, arrangements for their passage back to Trapani were complete. On January 25, 1910, the Adragna family and crew said their goodbyes to the gracious people of Ship Bottom who had helped them survive their tragedy. They were thankful for all that was done for them, but could not help feeling a little sadness when they left their new friends behind. There was a lot of emotion on the beach that day as hugs and tears were shared between the victims and their rescuers.

For several months, the salvaging company who now owned the *Fortuna* placed guards to stand watch over the ship to prevent people from stripping her clean. Several of the life boats had already disappeared, as had the ship's wheel. Personal belongings that had spilled from the ship onto the beach were eagerly snatched up by interested tourists. But, as a whole, the ship remained fairly intact for a number of years while the salvaging operation proceeded at an on-again, off-again pace. The abandoned ship was a wonderful place for children to play, climbing on the sideways deck, and hanging from the masts and spars and sometimes getting caught in the rigging which still hung from the poles.

The work of the salvagers was slow and tedious. They used torches to cut the metal hull into smaller pieces that could be transported by train or boat to the mainland. After many years of working on and off as time and money permitted, all that remained of the *Fortuna* was a skeleton of iron ribs. As the surf continued to wash sand upon the wreck, the ribs were buried so deep that no one would ever have known they were there.

Over the years, the *Fortuna* became just a story of the ship that wrecked on the beach in Ship Bottom during a severe winter storm. The stranded victims were gone, and all traces of the ship were gone, too. That fateful night of January 18, 1910, when the *Fortuna* ran aground remained only in the documented reports of the lifesaving stations, and in the memories of the people who helped care for its victims. And, as everyday life consumed their daily routines, their memories faded and were rapidly replaced by others. As the years passed by, storms would come and go, some so severe that the beach would erode, revealing the skeleton of an old sailing vessel. Beachcombers who came upon the skeleton and stopped to examine the remains would wonder. Unfamiliar with the real story of the *Fortuna*, they might simply make up their own story, envisioning a gallant ship that was caught in a storm and became another victim of the infamous and dangerous Barnegat Shoals.

As a teenager, Jerry Sprague went aboard the Fortuna
while it was stranded on the beach.

When the *Fortuna* ran aground, many local residents joined in the rescue operation. One of those who helped was Jerry Sprague, then a resident of Beach Haven. Although many years had passed since he stood on the decks of the ship, he remembered the details of both the incident and shipping in the early part of the century. In my interview with Jerry, age ninety-two in 1984, he offered the following details:

> *It was two days after the wreck on the beach in Ship Bottom that I became involved with the* Fortuna. *We followed all the wrecks. My uncle was a wrecking agent in Beach Haven and as soon as the word came that a ship was aground, the surf boat went in. Around here, my dad was*

known as the best handler of boats which were launched through the surf. As a matter of fact, all our tools and most of our dishes and blankets came from the stranded ships we salvaged.

A few days after the Fortuna *came aground at 16th Street in Ship Bottom, Father Whalen, the Catholic priest who was the Rector of St. Thomas Aquinas, asked me to help him get to the ship to deliver a Mass to the stranded crew. We went to Ship Bottom by train from Beach Haven where we lived. The Father and I walked right up to the ship at low tide without even getting our feet wet! That was because the ship was in ballast, meaning that she was light and was pushed up on the beach resting on a near even keel. We climbed the Jacob's ladder and met the first mate and crew which numbered twelve. The Father held a service - they were all Catholics - which they appreciated very much. Father Whalen could speak some Italian, but I could not so I used signs. I looked the ship over, climbed the rigging and saw the two anchors hanging in chain. I took special notice of anchors because when I was little I was an anchor boy, but I'll tell you more about that later.*

When the ship first grounded, the lifesaving crew informed the captain that they were removing the crew from the doomed ship and would house them at the lifesaving station. The captain threw up his hands and screamed 'No. No. They steal-a-my-ship!' He had probably heard about the Barnegat pirates on the New Jersey coast. The thing that struck me most was the difference in appearance between the first mate and his crew. The first mate was a very fine looking gentleman, very young, rather fair-skinned with a faint moustache. He was an aristocrat. But the crew, they were piratical-looking with dark skin, piercing jet black eyes, and all of them needed a shave! They wore heavy blouses, trousers with legs tucked into knee-high leather boots, and kerchiefs tied on their heads and around their necks. Each wore a belt with a knife around his waist. They all carried their knives, like in pictures of Robert Louis Stevenson's pirates!

We looked around a bit but didn't get into the hold - it was still battened down. There was a net under the bowsprit so when the men had to go out there, if they fell they would be caught by the net. I didn't see any tiles though, but I heard about them afterwards. We then climbed down the Jacob's ladder and returned to Beach Haven. Two days later I made the trip back to the ship by myself for another look around. The crew remembered me and let me aboard. I climbed the rigging again and inspected the anchors which were still in place hanging in their chain. The lifesaving station still had positioned a member of their crew on board to keep watch. He got into the wine and this spoiled my trip, more or less. By the time I arrived, he had too much to drink and got rather rambunctious. All of a sudden the first mate blew his whistle and twelve men popped out of the woodwork with their piercing eyes looking at me! I didn't like the looks of things so I jumped over the rail, went down the ladder and headed home before getting the chance to really look around.

Several days later the tide was again high and rough, causing the Fortuna *to be tossed about in the surf. She turned broadside to the beach and on January 22 fell over on her side, portside to the ocean. She was declared a total loss and was sold to salvagers as scrap. I never saw the ship again until my third trip in August. At that time it was lying on its side, but there were no anchors. What I think happened is this: When she rolled over, the port anchor was probably cut loose and sank so deep it never could be found. The starboard anchor was on top and the salvagers probably got that one.*

It was rumored on the beach about ten days later that the captain had committed suicide in grief over losing his ship. I never knew if it was true, though I don't see how he could do it with a wife and a new baby. [A newspaper article in a scrapbook on display in the Beach Haven Museum confirms this rumor.]

I don't have a tangible souvenir of the Fortuna, just memories. I've heard there are people who saved the wheel and masts and perhaps other items, too. I guess I didn't have the foresight to take any. But Mrs. Sprague [the former Evelyn Broome of Beach Haven who Sprague married in 1927] has one - a memorable dinner. A friend of hers had befriended the captain's wife and she was made a present of some tomato paste from the ship. It was the first time they had a spaghetti dinner - real Italian, too!

The Fortuna *was the only steel, square-rigged sailing ship to wreck on Long Beach Island that I know of. But, I do remember other wrecks. At the time of the wreck of the Fortuna there was not much in Ship Bottom, just some shacks owned by the lifesaving crew for use by their families during the summer months. But there were a lot of us Spragues around the Island back then. There was my great grandfather, Jeremiah. He was the keeper of Barnegat Lighthouse at one time [1841-46]. That was for the old lighthouse, the one which washed away first. My grandfather, Jeremiah's son, was the captain of the Beach Haven Terrace Lifesaving Station for twenty-five years. Then there was my father, widely known as the best bayman in the area. He was one of many who used to take charter boats out of Beach Haven filled with fishermen. When it was time for the boats to dock, I would row out in my rowboat and help them set their anchor. I was known as an anchor boy and for each anchor I set I was paid a nickel. That's how I got to know so much about anchors.*

It would be really exciting to locate the baby who was taken from the stranded ship. It is probably the only person alive, besides me, who has ever been aboard the Fortuna. *You can bet I will be at the dedication ceremonies for the anchor. Aside from my great interest in local history, just you try to keep me away from anything having to do with an anchor!*

(Jerry Sprague - 1984)

The Fortuna was driven ashore during a violent storm
on January 18, 1910. Five days later she fell over into
the surf and was declared a total loss.

Old photos of Fortuna wreck, 16th Street, Ship Bottom, NJ

(Compliments of Unshredded Nostalgia, Barnegat NJ)

Ship Bottom Lifesavers, Station No. 20 (1908)

L to R, Top Row: Torrow, Brad Salmons, (?), Long John Cranmer, (?)
Bottom Row: (?), Jim Henry Cranmer, Bart Pharo, J. Horace Cranmer,
Caleb Conklin, Captain Ike Truex, station dog, Tippy

Practice drill launching the surfboat.

THE Italian Bark "Fortuna" from Trapani, Sicily, in ballast for New York by way of Barbadoes, ran aground near Beach Haven about 2.30 on the morning of January 1", 1910. The captain, Adrigua G. Battista, lost his bearings owing to the foggy weather. He has since committed suicide from brooding over the loss of his vessel and the consequent cancelling of his commission as a sailing master.

The vessel is built of iron, is about 40 years old, and was two months out from her home port. She carried a crew of 13 men, and also had on board the captain's wife and three children; the youngest having been born after leaving Trapani. No one was lost; all on board were rescued at daybreak by the crew of the life saving station.

When the vessel was washed up on the beach into its present position there were three pigs found in the stern on a pile of rigging—hungry but none the worse for their experience.

The Fortuna is now being dismantled for junk, but the hull will no doubt remain an interesting feature of the beach for some time to come.

One of several reportings that Captain Adragna
committed suicide in 1910

Searching for lost treasure will always be a challenge for if it were so easy to recover, it would have already been found.

April - 1983

It was almost time for the school's spring break when we began to think about where to spend our vacation. The worst of winter had already passed, and the balmy days of April showed some promise. Greg had a business trip scheduled for that week so the kids and I opted to open up the beach house and spend the week on Long Beach Island. Alison, age fifteen, had a project to complete over the vacation and thought that mixing a little fun while working on her project would suit her just fine. Besides, she was looking forward to seeing her friends who lived on the Island year-round. Amanda, age ten, was looking forward to exploring the Island, off season. And since Jonathan was only five, he did whatever we told him to do.

Long Beach Island in 1983 was nothing like the way it was in 1910. In the early 1900s, the Island, eighteen miles long and just a few blocks wide, had just two resort communities that flourished: Beach Haven at the southern end, and Barnegat Light to the north. The space in-between was pretty desolate. In the late 1950s, the opening of the Garden State Parkway brought thousands of people to the Island to spend their summer vacations at one of New Jersey's prime seashore communities. Many fell in love with the beauty of the Jersey Shore, and, almost instantly, the Island was dotted with thousands of summer cottages. While the Island exploded with vacationers during the summer months, come Labor Day, the tourist season was over and most of the shops closed down for the winter. This scarcity of people living on Long Beach Island during the off season made it almost feel like it was still 1910.

The temperature was in the high sixties the day we arrived at our beach house, unseasonably warm for April. It was a pleasant change from the many snowstorms we'd had the past winter season. Though the sea was calm, the beach showed telltale signs of severe weather conditions. Serious erosion had formed steep cliffs that dropped four to five feet to the ocean below. The beach was littered with thousands of shells that had loosened from their ocean beds and washed ashore. Overnight, the temperature plummeted to below freezing and the wind howled, rattling the windows and causing the curtains to flutter from the draft. It looked like we were in for a real Nor'easter. But, as quickly as the wind arrived it quieted down giving way to a beautiful, peaceful snowfall.

When the weather at the shore is pleasant, it's a real delight to get out and walk on the beach. But there are times when it is better to just stay inside and keep warm. To me, this seemed to be one of those times. But it came as no surprise to me when Amanda and her friend, Kristen, reasoned that a vacation at the beach meant you went on the beach, regardless of the weather. Bundled in winter parkas, mittens, earmuffs and hats, they were dressed for the elements, much like the lifesavers of years ago. They were well-prepared for the cold when they headed out the door to walk the beach.

Several hours had passed since they disappeared behind the dune and, except for the fact that I knew how adventurous Amanda was, I might have started to worry. If Amanda had been given a middle name, it would have been "Adventurer" spelled with a capital 'A'. She could always be found doing something unusual and, at times, skirting the outer edges of danger. She once spent an entire day climbing on the sharp slippery rocks of the jetties catching crabs for supper, only to release them when she learned that they had to be dropped into boiling water to cook them.

Before long I spotted the two girls way in the distance, dragging a large bag of beach treasures behind them. By the time they reached the house they were exhausted, but the excitement of their adventure gave them a second wind.

"You'll never guess what we found," Amanda blurted out between gasps of frozen breath.

I tried to peel off her clothes that were frozen stiff like cardboard, but she was too excited about showing me the treasures in the bag to offer any degree of cooperation. She opened the bag and dumped its contents on the kitchen floor: snow, sand, shells and.......

"Amanda! Where did you get all those tiles? There must be twenty or thirty of them," I questioned. Wow! Their collection was impressive. Oh, I was soooo jealous! I almost wished that I'd been the one to brave the cold to discover the mother lode. But I hadn't. Instead, I listened to the recap of their trip with envy.

Amanda continued telling her story. "We walked about two miles up towards Ship Bottom by the water tower. We found most of them by the shipwreck. You should bring your camera up there to take some pictures."

"Yeah, it's some ugly old metal thing," Kristen added, not at all impressed with the whole discovery.

I gathered my camera gear and drove with Amanda and Kristen to the beach where the wreck was located. I was not prepared for the sight that lay before me. I was expecting to find the wreck of a Chris Craft or other small pleasure boat that had been battered against the rock jetty.

"There it is. See, I told you it was ugly." Kristen reiterated.

"This is the wreck you found all those tiles by?" I asked one more time, just to be sure there was no misunderstanding.

"Yeah, right here. See those things sticking out of the sand that look like a skeleton? It's really big, like a dinosaur. I think it's the skeleton of an old shipwreck," Amanda observed pointing out the curved lines of the ship's rusted hull.

Immediately I knew. The rusty pieces of metal formed the perfect outline of a big ship. The location was perfect, right at the water's edge on the 16th Street beach. I looked around and saw the "Danger-Wreck- No Bathing" sign that was posted back by the dune. It just had to be. My mind began to wander back to the information that I had already researched. "The *Fortuna* came in hard and fast on an even keel, beaching herself on the sand at the water's edge. After several days she turned broadside to the beach and fell over into the churning surf. Salvagers removed the parts of the wreck that were above the sand, leaving the remains buried under the sand." That confirmed, without question, these were the remains of the *Fortuna*, the only ship to ever wreck on the 16th Street beach in Ship Bottom. How fortunate for me that so many red tiles would surface at that very same spot after so many years, and that Amanda and Kristen were there to find them. Aunt Lydie was right. She had seen them at the sight of the wreck of the *Fortuna* seventy-three years before, and here they were again, scattered all over the same beach.

A chilling wind started to kick up as the light of day disappeared behind the dune, taking the warmth of the sun along with it. Though shivering from the excitement and extreme cold, I managed to hold the camera still long enough to take a few pictures. It was then time to call it a day. We headed back to the house to make some hot chocolate to help thaw our frozen bodies.

I could hardly wait to share the news of my discovery. I called home that night and told Greg the story of our incredible find. Although he listened politely and sounded somewhat pleased, he was not as excited as I thought he would, or even should be. He most likely thought I was jumping to conclusions, thinking this was the wreck of the *Fortuna*. My sheer optimism was not that convincing. I needed something more tangible to prove to him that these were the *Fortuna's* remains.

As the weekend approached, the weather warmed up to be more typical for April. We took many more walks on the beach looking and hoping to find more tiles, but we didn't find any. Not a single one! How disappointing was that! Amanda and Kristen must have gathered all that had washed ashore, while the ocean kept those that never made it through the surf onto the beach.

When we heard Greg's car pull in the driveway on Saturday morning, the kids and I surrounded it like swarming insects. "Don't take your coat off. Let's go look at the shipwreck we found," we pleaded, racing towards the beach. After a slight hesitation to catch his breath, we started our walk to 16th Street in Ship Bottom. We walked two miles north, passing the familiar jetties that marked the route. When we spotted the tall blue water tower, we knew we'd arrived at the right spot.

As rapidly as the action of the surf had eroded the beach exposing the wreck, it was possible that the sand could have buried the wreck again. The powerful surf moves tons of sand around with each passing tide. But, as we topped the rise at the 14th Street beach, we could see the wreck in the distance. It was still there. The tide was low and the skeleton of the *Fortuna* was visible at the edge of the water. The shape was unmistakable. No doubt this was the skeleton of a large ship. It measured about 190 feet from bow to stern, its jagged rusty iron ribs protruding three or four feet above the sand. In the slurry of the waves I could see the oak beam that connected the ribs. It was still in perfect condition. Wet from the ocean water, the finish looked as shiny as my kitchen table.

Until now, my *Fortuna* souvenir collection consisted of red tiles and photographs. I desperately wanted to have a piece of the ship to add to my growing collection. I tried to break off a little piece of an iron rib, but it was too thick. I couldn't even break off one tiny piece. The *Fortuna's* skeleton remained intact.

As we waded ankle deep through the icy cold surf to inspect the skeletal remains of the ship, I found convincing evidence that this was, indeed, the *Fortuna*. Embedded in the iron framework of the vessel were pieces of red tiles still bearing the partial inscription of its French manufacturer: "Arnaud Eti," "enry, Marseil." The very same tiles loaded into the hold of the *Fortuna* as ballast before she left port in Marseille in 1909. The evidence was overwhelming: the location of the wreck at 16th Street and now the pieces of tile stuck to it. Without question, *this was the remains of the* Fortuna.

There I was, standing beside a ship that wrecked seventy-three years ago, still not grasping the importance of my discovery. I never was much of a history buff, but then again, I had never been this close to history before. Until now, I thought I knew all there was to know about the *Fortuna*. I knew by heart the story from "The Lure of Long Beach," once considered the bible of Long Beach Island's history. I'd memorized the paragraph found on Page 64:

> *One of the most picturesque wrecks of comparatively recent times was that of the gallant Italian bark* Fortuna, *a steel ship which was driven ashore at Ship Bottom in a terrific storm during the winter of 1909-10. She came in hard and fast on an even keel and the crew of the Ship Bottom Life Saving Station rescued all on board, including a newly born baby, a pig and a cat. Her home port was Trapani in Sicily.*
> "The Lure of Long Beach"
> By Charles Edgar Nash
> Copyright 1936 by The Long Beach Board of Trade

In my collection of artifacts, I had several photographs of the stranded ship as pictured in local maritime books. I even had pieces of the ballast that she spilled upon our shores when she ran aground. And now, to be standing alongside the remaining ribs of this historic shipwreck. What more could I possibly ask for?

I didn't ask for much. All I wanted was just one more chance to photograph the wreck up close before it disappeared beneath the sand again. That chance came the next day, on Sunday morning, at the time of low tide. I walked among the ribs taking close-up pictures of shells, fishing line and tiles that were stuck to the ribs. Waves rushed through the rusty cutouts of the frame. Click. Spray splashed over the three biggest ribs at the bow's end. Click. The oak beam connecting the ribs glistened, wet and shiny from a recent wave. Click. Click. Click. I was about to turn off my camera when I saw it. What was causing that rippling effect in the water as it passed over the object just off the bow?

"Greg, over here. Quick. I see something out there. Just past the bow. It looks like, like a cannonball. Here, hold my camera," I said as I removed the strap from around my neck. "I'm going to get it to add to my collection of *Fortuna* items." The water was extremely cold, but I darted through the surf not really caring. I reached for the object, hoping to grab it before getting totally drenched by an incoming wave. I wrapped my hands securely around it and tried to lift, but it wouldn't budge. After the wave receded, I tried again to lift it, again without success. After several more futile attempts, I left the frigid water, shivering but still determined. With numbing toes and fingers, I entered the surf for another try. I grabbed onto the ball, and this time could feel that it was not just a ball sitting on the sand, but was attached to something beneath the water. Something that felt like a pole or metal bar. I spotted Greg back on shore removing his sneakers in preparation to come offer his opinion and assistance. It is appropriate to mention at this point that Greg is not particularly fond of water much below seventy degrees. With the water temperature hovering around the thirty-six degree mark, I knew it to be a gesture of love that brought him into the water at all.

"Let's see what you've got there," Greg said as reached over to inspect the object I was so determined to retrieve. "You're right. It is attached to something. It goes down quite deep." He stood up and turned around to survey the area. First he looked at the round object, then at its relationship to the outline of the ship's ribs. He knew right away what the object was, and knew the likelihood that I would be adding it to my collection was slim to none.

"Look at the ribs. Now look at where your cannonball is. This is no cannonball," he pointed out. And at exactly the same moment, we both said out loud, "This is the anchor from this ship."

"The anchor from the *Fortuna*? From MY ship, the *Fortuna*?" I kept saying over and over again. I felt so excited, like a kid who had just discovered her stocking on Christmas morning. Already my thoughts had jumped from owning a mere cannonball to having a gigantic anchor. Just as I had visions of plucking the ball from the surf, I had dreams of digging a little sand from around this anchor and lifting it up and trucking it home to display on my front lawn. Yes, dreams they were. I knew the anchor from the *Fortuna* was not likely to be a small one. A ship her size would have carried at least one big anchor, most likely, two. I wondered how on earth I would get it out of the sand.

We began to talk about the obstacles. We would need a big crane to lift it out, and surely we didn't have one of those in our fleet of vehicles. Besides, the beach where the anchor is located is not our property. It's public land. How could we get permission to dig up public property to remove someone else's anchor and keep it for ourselves? And, what about Ship Bottom? The *Fortuna* was a wreck of such historic importance to the town, surely they would never allow someone to just dig it up and take it away. The more we talked about the recovery of the *Fortuna*'s anchor, the more it became apparent that we could not, and should not, recover it for ourselves. Again, we both came up with the same idea.

"We can recover the anchor and give it to the town of Ship Bottom," we both said, congratulating ourselves for solving the problem of what to do with the anchor. "The anchor really should stay in Ship Bottom." The *Fortuna* is a part of their history. Even the fire and police departments depict the image of the fallen *Fortuna* on their shields. One thing led to another and our thoughts grew more elaborate as the day progressed. What if we could get the anchor and preserve it? We could then turn it over to the town of Ship Bottom. They could build a monument in the center of town to represent the maritime history of Long Beach Island. And, it could be dedicated to all those who ever sailed these waters and as a tribute to those who lost their lives in the hundreds of shipwrecks off our coast.

Before we even had a plan to remove the anchor from the sand, our thoughts began to grow. We didn't even know if it was complete. Was there more to it than just the ball and two feet of pole we could feel under the water? Or was it just a broken remnant left behind by the salvagers? If the anchor was complete, could it be freed or was it tangled up with other parts of the remaining wreck? To a salvager, an anchor was worth its weight in gold. The salvagers may have left it behind because it was twisted in the iron frame of the ship and couldn't be pulled out. But the bigger question remained: if the anchor were intact and able to be recovered, who had the right to claim it?

The following weekend I caught sight of Herbert Marvin coming up the street towards the beach for his early morning swim. Mr. Marvin, a retired lawyer, had come from Philadelphia for many years to spend weekends at Wida's Hotel on 44th Street in Brant Beach. Though in his early seventies, his tall lean build was testimony to his healthy lifestyle. I interrupted his path.

"Mr. Marvin, how are you this morning?" I greeted him, stopping him in his tracks. We exchanged pleasantries, inquiring about each other's week, sharing a mutual hope that the water had warmed up enough for a swim. He noted that while he did have a good week, he was sure that a weekend in Brant Beach would be better, admitting he was due for a change of pace.

"Well, what have you been up to this week, Carole," he inquired, hoping I had something interesting to report.

"Oh, my gosh. I've been up to quite a bit," I responded as I filled him in on the details of my find. I was hoping that, as a lawyer, he could be of some help so I asked him, "Do you know anything about maritime law? I was wondering what claim I would have on this anchor."

"Well, that's not my field, and I would hesitate to even guess because the law changes so much from week to week. But I do have a friend I can ask. He will know. He specializes in maritime law," he answered, eager to be of some assistance. "I'll let you know next weekend when I come down."

The week dragged by much too slowly as I waited for word from Mr. Marvin. When we came back to the beach house the following weekend, I visited the site of the partially buried anchor, just to make sure it was still there. And, it was. The tides were running a bit higher than usual, keeping the exposed ball of the anchor slightly under the water even at dead low tide. For the time being I did not have to worry about anyone else finding my anchor and claiming it for themselves. I had time to wait for the official word from Mr. Marvin.

Saturday morning, just like clockwork, Mr. Marvin headed up to the beach for his early morning swim. Of course I was at the curb to greet him when he reached our house. I think I wished him "good morning" though I'm not really sure. Selfishly, I bombarded him with my question: "Do you have any news for me?"

"Well, yes I have," he replied in a very formal, lawyer-like manner. "I spoke with my friend. He's very much up on maritime law, and he says that in New Jersey, the law is 'finders-keepers' so you can claim it for yourself if you want to. He was concerned about how you were going to recover it, but once you overcame that hurdle, there's nothing to say that the anchor does not belong to you."

"That's great news! Can you come with us? I want to show you what I found, and exactly where it is," I begged as he joined me and Greg on our walk. The two mile walk was no challenge for Mr. Marvin, an avid beach walker. It was a struggle for us to keep up with him, though we managed and before long reached the spot where I found the anchor just a week before. It was low tide, and I could see that viewing conditions would be just perfect.

"Right here is the entire outline of the hull of the *Fortuna*," I pointed out as we wandered closer to inspect the ribs of the wreck. I could see he was quite impressed. I did not know it at the time, but Mr. Marvin was a history buff, and antiques-minded, as well. I could see he was thrilled to play a small role in the rebirth of the *Fortuna*. More importantly, he was anxious to see the elusive anchor that was now a part of his life, too.

"This is the stern, up there is the bow. See how the ribs curve? And, when the water washes out, you can see the oak beam that holds it all together. Look, there it is," I shouted as the tide receded revealing the beauty of the entire skeleton.

"What a spectacular sight," he remarked, excited to be seeing it in person. "Now, where is this anchor you told me about?"

"It's up at the bow end, right where you would expect a ship to drop anchor," I said projecting a great deal of self-imposed authority. "But, we have to be patient. You have to wait for the water to go out before you can catch a glimpse of it. Oh, over there! Right now. Look. Just in the white foam of that wave. That thing that looks like a cannonball is the anchor. That's it!" As he gazed in the general direction, I could tell he was disappointed. I am sure he expected to see the entire anchor just sitting there waiting for me to claim it and carry it home.

"What do you mean, that's it? What's it? Where? I don't see anything," he said, still wondering if I really had found anything at all.

"Okay," I patiently replied. "When the next wave goes out, we can get a closer look. Over there, about ten to twelve feet off the last protruding rib. When the water washes over the ball it creates a ripple effect. Do you see it? That's the piece of the anchor."

"I see the ball, alright, but I don't understand how you can know it's an anchor. It doesn't look like one to me," he argued. He needed to be convinced. Greg picked up a piece of broken snow fencing and began to draw a diagram in the wet sand to illustrate the anchor's position.

"Here is the ball we just spotted. It's on this part of the anchor, on the end of the cross piece called the stock. The stock is attached to the main body called the shank, and the flukes, the parts that grab the sand when the anchor is set, stand approximately like this," Greg explained as he carefully drew the pieces of the anchor to help Mr. Marvin visualize our treasure. "We can't be sure if the whole anchor is there or not, but knowing that anchors are made to last, I'd be willing to bet it's intact. After all, it's a German anchor, you know."

"Well, if you say so. But I was expecting to see more of it before reaching the conclusion that this was an anchor. But, then again, I don't know much about this sort of thing. Guess I will have to take your word for it. At any rate, as far as the law is concerned, if you found it, and you want it, you can claim it for your own," Mr. Marvin stated, knowing that I was more interested in the law than I was in convincing him that this was indeed an anchor. I thanked him for contacting his friend regarding the laws of maritime discoveries in New Jersey and promised I would acknowledge him in my book. He was both delighted to be of help and to be a part of the story. I took a picture of him standing beside the skeleton of the *Fortuna* before we headed back to Brant Beach. As we retraced our steps, I gave Mr. Marvin the whole history of the wreck of the *Fortuna*. I could tell that he was hooked on the story and my newly discovered anchor. He complimented me for extensively researching the *Fortuna* and assured me that if anyone could pull it off, it would be me. It was reassuring to have an outside party express confidence in the outcome of the project. I knew there would be many times down the road that I would cling to those few early words of encouragement.

Exercising our confidence in New Jersey's finders-keepers law regarding items from the sea, Greg stamped the words "claimed for Ship Bottom 5/2/83 by Carole Bradshaw " on a heavy metal bar and padlocked it to the exposed stock of the anchor. Officially, I was the proud owner of the *Fortuna's* anchor.

In less than a week, the sand that had washed away to expose a portion of the anchor washed back onto the beach, completely covering it. A few days later, the ocean re-deposited tons of sand on the 16th Street beach, covering the skeletal remains of the *Fortuna*. She had disappeared beneath the sand. The *Fortuna* was completely gone.

First sighting of exposed anchor ball, April 1983

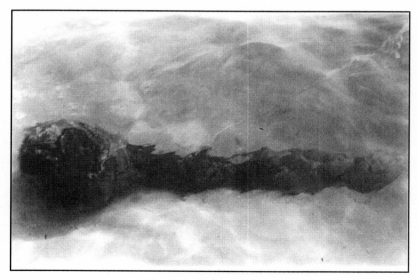

Ball and stock of anchor as seen underwater.

People who say it cannot be done should not interrupt those who are doing it.

Bernard Shaw

Summer - 1983

It was easy to determine the future home of the *Fortuna's* anchor. It was so obvious, at least to me. The famous wreck of the *Fortuna* happened in Ship Bottom, and it is a well documented part of their history. Yes, its future was obvious; the anchor should stay in Ship Bottom. But just because I thought it would be perfect for Ship Bottom to display the anchor didn't mean the town would share the same enthusiasm. I needed to let them know about my discovery so they could decide for themselves.

> May 2, 1983
> Office of the Mayor
> Ship Bottom, New Jersey
>
> Dear Mayor Nissen,
> Every once in a while, we have the good fortune of having a real treasure fall right into our lap - and that is what is happening right now!
> I have recently discovered the anchor from the *Fortuna,* a prominent wreck which occurred in your town of Ship Bottom nearly a century ago. What an historic find! It's something you can use to enrich the maritime history of Ship Bottom.
> I am hoping you have an interest in removing this piece of history from its location in the waters off Long Beach Island and placing it in a prominent place in your town. A simple structure could house this approximately 9 foot anchor, making it a real attraction in Ship Bottom, The Gateway to Long Beach Island. What the Lucy Evelyn did for Beach Haven, this anchor could do for Ship Bottom. 3

I know this sounds mysterious, but there are reasons for not disclosing all my information at this time. I have no monetary or commercial intentions - I do not plan to "offer for sale" a map to its location. I merely wish, however, to let you know of its presence in the hope that you and your Council will want to follow up on the action to turn a bit of Island history into a piece of reality for everyone to enjoy. I do not believe history should be bought or sold, merely used to share with those who are interested in reliving part of the past. The news of its location might send many a merchant to its resting place, ready to extract it and put up for sale for a fast buck. If you do not have any interest in securing this anchor for the purpose of public display, then I will keep my secret to myself and let the anchor remain in the sea where she was laid to rest seventy three years ago.

Members of our immediate family have been summer residents of Long Beach Island since 1940, with other island acquaintances, still living, going back before 1900. One vividly recalls the wreck. That's a lot of years to have shared with LBI. We've taken a lot of good memories out of LBI - and now we have a chance to give something back.

I can be reached most afternoons at [phone number] or by letter at the above address. I am hoping you will seek additional information for I truly think this display would be a great addition to the town of Ship Bottom.

Very truly yours,
Carole Bradshaw

I mailed the letter and waited. Two weeks went by and not a word from the mayor. Perhaps the letter had been misdirected? I called to inquire.

"Hello, Mayor Nissen?" I asked in a questioning tone. "My name is Carole Bradshaw and I recently wrote you a proposal to"

"Yes, I'm glad you called," he answered. "I've been holding your letter, the one about the anchor. Quite frankly, I'm not sure what to do about it. Of course I am enthusiastic about getting the anchor. Do you really think we'd be able to get it out?"

"To be truthful, it's a gamble, but it's a chance that would be too great to pass up," I answered, hoping I sounded convincing without forcing the issue. "I think we could get enough volunteers together who would be interested in helping out, and I really think we could do it, don't you? The anchor is located at the surf line, almost always under water, except during an extremely low tide. You know, like the one we get in late September at the time of the autumnal equinox."

"Well, yes, I don't think the manpower would be a problem. Why I know the fire department would be glad to help out. And you could ask Art Cox. He would probably get his big crane to lift it out." Mayor Nissen had just crossed over the line from being curious to envisioning the anchor already on display in the center of his town.

"Okay, as long as you have an interest in recovering it, then what's the next thing we have to do to get the ball rolling?" I questioned, not wanting to waste another minute's time.

"The first thing we must do is to get approval from Council to remove it from the sand. And then we need their approval to display it in front of the Borough Hall building," Mayor Nissen replied, already mapping out in his mind the spot for its location. "We have a Council meeting coming up this Tuesday. Would you be ready to make a proposal to them at that meeting?"

"Would I be ready? I sure would," I quickly responded, forgetting that the one thing I disliked most was speaking in front of a large group of people.

By now the anchor had vanished, buried about a foot beneath the sand. Fortunately, Greg had taken careful measurements documenting its exact location so we would be sure to find it when the time came for the recovery effort. 'Standing on the 16th Street beach, facing east towards the ocean, pace off 117.6 feet due east of the lower piling, seven feet north of inside corner piling under third window north on house.' With these measurements, the anchor was always within reach even if it was totally out of sight.

*   *   *   *   *

Tuesday's Council meeting was attended by fifteen members, and the order of business proceeded as laid out on the agenda. I looked out over the audience for a familiar face and found only one: Tom Oakley of the Public Works Department. It was very comforting to see a friendly face. Although I recognized the names of several others, mainly from reading about them in the local newspapers, they were still strangers. Before the meeting adjourned, I was introduced and given the floor to present my proposal to the Council.

My name is Carole Bradshaw, and I am here to make a proposal for you to acquire something that I found on one of your beaches. Over the years, there have been hundreds of shipwrecks here on Long Beach Island, many of them occurring in or near Ship Bottom. One of the most famous was that of the *Fortuna* which ran aground right up the street in 1910 during a violent storm. All lives were saved, including a newborn baby. The parts of the ship that the salvagers could not cart away remained on the beach and are buried beneath the sand. Over the years, from time to time, the ruins of the *Fortuna* would come and go as storms washed away the sand. I've heard from many a surfer of the painful gashes inflicted on their shins when they hit the invisible ribs just under the surface of the water. This past winter, severe beach erosion exposed the ship's skeleton again, and along with it, a real treasure: the ship's anchor. I know where this anchor is, and if you would give me permission to organize the efforts to recover it from beneath the sand, I will donate it to the town of Ship Bottom for you to display in front of the Borough Hall."

A heightened buzz of chatter filled the room, silenced by the words of volunteer fireman Dudbridge Taylor. "Well, it sounds like a good idea to me."

"I'm not at all sure you can even get it out. That's a whale of a job," objected council member Bill Stillwell. "You would have to build a caisson around it, and that would take a lot of money, more money than I think you would want to spend. How much money are you asking for, anyway?" questioned Stillwell.

"I'm not here to ask you for money. I'm asking for your permission and support to organize the attempt to recover it. I don't think we'd have any trouble getting volunteers to help out," I declared in my most convincing voice.

The members of the council continued a brief discussion and, with the exception of Mr. Stillwell, all agreed to grant me permission. Mr. Stillwell finally came around and cautiously stated, "If you really think you can do it, then you can go ahead and try, but I don't think you'll ever get it out."

I did not need his endorsement, just his permission. I must have had an honest face and a convincing story. Mayor Nissen stated that he "considered the proposed project worthwhile, and that the recovery of the anchor would be a fitting complement to the 1985 observances marking the 60th anniversary of the borough's founding." With the unanimous agreement of the Ship Bottom Borough Council to grant me permission to organize the efforts to recover the anchor of the *Fortuna*, I was ready to start the project.

My closing words, "Thank you very much for granting me your permission and having the foresight to recover this anchor. I hope that by the end of the summer you will all get to see the anchor for yourself," were lost in a frenzy of activity. It was immediately apparent that most of the strangers in the audience were from the media. Within minutes, the reporters were thirsting for more details: "Where is the anchor? Is this the shipwreck that gave Ship Bottom its name? How do you plan to raise the anchor? Who do you expect to help?" I answered the questions as best I could: "The anchor is located beneath the sand near the remains of the ship from which it was lost. No, it is not the wreck which gave Ship Bottom its name. The anchor can probably be raised with the use of a crane. As for manpower, we will accept everyone who wishes to volunteer, and I plan to be the first one there with a shovel!"

I thought the meeting went exceptionally well, especially since I offered no proof that the anchor really existed. And they never asked for any. With luck, it would not be long before the *Fortuna's* anchor would be resting outside the Ship Bottom Borough Hall, right down the same street from where it was lost seventy-three years before.

A short while after the Council meeting, Herb Josephson of A&H Printing in Ship Bottom offered to make me business cards to get me out there to "spread the word." When he later presented me with my cards, I saw that he had given me the title "The Anchor Lady." And the name has stuck ever since.

The following day, the *Asbury Park Press* flashed the headlines: "Woman Seeks Advice to Salvage Anchor," and with a fair degree of accuracy reported the events of the previous night's Council meeting. The *Press of Atlantic City* carried a similar story: "Town Uncovers Anchor from its Past." Officially, the word was out. Before noon, a number of townspeople had already called the borough clerk asking how they could help.

I followed up on Mayor Nissen's suggestion to contact Art Cox to see if we could use his crane to pull the anchor from the sand. I described the project to him, and he seemed interested. "Bob Nissen tells me you have a huge crane that would be able to lift a very heavy anchor," I told Art, the quiet man on the other end of the phone. He was a man of few words and merely offered, "Yes, I think it can do the job."

Not sure if that was a yes or a no, I continued. "Would you be willing to donate the use of your crane to lift out the *Fortuna's* anchor?"

"Yes, I would like to help out where I can," he responded.

"Would you be available sometime in late September?" I asked.

"Sure, that would be fine," he replied.

Mayor Nissen was right when he said, "Art is quiet by nature, with not much to say for himself. But he is a darn good, dependable worker. When he says he will do a job, he puts his all into it. His family has done a lot for the town of Ship Bottom, always there to help out without regard to the cost or expenditure of hard labor." His credentials were impressive. I added a few more sentences to the conversation just to make it last a minute or so longer, and then thanked him before hanging up the phone. It was exciting to have our first real volunteer, and by donating his time and equipment, we were prepared to handle the biggest part of the project. To Art, it was no big deal. There was something that needed to be done, and he could do it, so he would. It's just the way he was.

The raising of the anchor was scheduled to take place in September when the tourist season would be over and the beaches free of summer sunbathers. After consulting the calendar, we chose the time during the autumnal equinox when tides would be at their lowest. The recovery was set for Tuesday, September 20, 1983.

During the course of the summer, I continued to walk the beach, searching for and finding more red tiles. I grew more excited with every piece I found - and I found many. No longer were they just meaningless pieces of interesting beach finds. They were now historic; already antiques. I noticed a funny thing, though. When I looked at the pile of tiles in my collection, there were no whole ones, only pieces ranging from tiny slivers up to about five inches. I once offered my children five dollars if they found a whole one, but they never did. My guess is that the tiles were too fragile to withstand the force of the waves that carried them ashore.

*   *   *   *   *

Monday's mail arrived at noon. I thanked the mailman for the daily collection of envelopes and casually looked through the pile. There were a few letters, a limited number of bills, and an airmail letter. For a quick moment, I wondered who was traveling abroad that would send me a letter. Without looking at the return address or postmark, I opened it.

> Dear Madame,
>
> We received your very interesting letter. In effect, for many years now, the society of Arnaud & Co had been absorbed by Marseille Tiles.
>
> The photos corresponding to the model of these tiles we received are no longer produced. Unfortunately, we no longer have any samples in stock which we'd be able to send you.
>
> This type of tile covering was used to cover the roofs under and along with other tiles not only in France but also in other foreign countries. We know the use of

these on homes existed in such countries as Singapore, Australia, Mexico and [throughout] Latin America.

It is, therefore, not surprising that an Italian boat leaving from Marseille had been bound for New Jersey. For your information, we attached a letterhead on which the Co. Arnaud is shown at the time the Society of Tiles of Marseille absorbed it. (The attached paper is a copy of an old paper - but none of these individual companies exist any longer.)

We hope this information will satisfy your demands. We wish you all the best and our sincerest regards, Madame.

> G.M. Zarifi
> Tuileries de Marseille et de la Mediterranee
> le President
> Directeur General
> S.A. Capital 8.077.100F.
> 4, Place Felix Baret - B.P. No 5-13251
> Marseille Cedex 6

After such a long silence, it seemed like too much of a coincidence that the letter should arrive at the same time I discovered the anchor. First there were the tiles, then the shipwreck. And now the anchor. All the pieces of this puzzling story kept landing right at my feet. Was it coincidence or was it fate?

Throughout the summer, our list of volunteers continued to grow. Many people offered to do their part; not for a chance to make the front page of the newspaper, or even to get something out of it for themselves, but because they wanted to be a part of something they believed in. George Powell headed the team of volunteer firemen who were planning to assist by using their fire hoses as a jet to remove the sand from around the anchor. He figured the force of the water's pressure would eat through the sand at a faster rate than anything else. He and his men would be ready. Art Cox said he would be ready with his crane on any date that we needed him, and would take care of assembling his own crew. Mayor Nissen would also be there to do whatever needed to be done. Most often, he was the smallest man present and would always be the first to lift the heaviest object, or get the dirtiest trying to get a job done. Hard work was no stranger to him. And, of course, I would not miss this day for the world! I did not plan to be just an observer; I would be there to pitch in wherever needed. And, of course, to witness the anchor being lifted from its seventy-three year resting place.

As the September date drew closer, I began to get nervous. I was not used to the laid-back way the Island people operated. Here it was less than a week before the scheduled recovery date, and we had never met as a group to discuss our plan. I contacted all the key players and scheduled a meeting for Sunday, September 18 at twelve o'clock noon, on the 16th Street beach in Ship Bottom.

As usual Greg and I, with our son Jonathan in tow, arrived early. Before the others showed up, I searched to see if by some stroke of good fortune the anchor had resurfaced. But it hadn't. It was still buried somewhere deep beneath the sand. Within minutes, the rest of the recovery crew began to arrive. Mayor Bob Nissen came with his son, Jan, a strong-looking, husky fellow who looked like he could almost lift the anchor without the help of a crane. George Powell arrived with several other firemen who planned to be on hand on the day of the anchor raising. Two unfamiliar young men, maybe in their late twenties, crossed over the dune and came forward to join our group.

"Hi, I'm Carole Bradshaw, the Anchor Lady," I introduced myself to the group. It was obvious to everyone that the two young men were new to the plan, and no one knew why they were there. I approached one of the men who then introduced himself to me.

"Hi. Paul Buterick," he said offering his hand in a strong, confident handshake. "I'll be using my crane to raise your anchor. Art Cox had trouble with his crane and asked me to fill in for him."

Well, that was not exactly how it was, but you wouldn't have heard it from Art Cox. As it was told to me, at the last minute Art's big crane was down and he could not get the part to fix it. He knew we were depending on him to do the job because he said he would. And, even though his crane was down, he still planned to follow through with his part of the deal. He took it upon himself to contact Buterick Bulkheading, a competitor no less, and offered to pay him to do the job that he himself could not. No fuss. No big deal. He just took care of it, quietly, behind the scene. When Art explained the details of the project to Paul, he was very intrigued and saw it as somewhat of a challenge. Of course he was interested in filling in. And, of course, Paul did not accept any money for the job. He volunteered his services, his crane and his crew, just like Art had done, determined to get the anchor raised.

We checked out the condition of the beach, the access route for the equipment and the location where we would start digging for the anchor. No one, not even once, questioned where the anchor was. No one walked up to the location where I said the anchor was buried or asked to see it. Yet, they were all willing to devote a whole day and a lot of expense to retrieve something not one of them had ever seen. They were there to raise an anchor that I said was there, so it must be there. I found this trust to be pretty amazing. I really began to feel the pressure to find the exact spot where the anchor was hidden beneath the sand.

In our meeting, Greg explained that he had carefully paced off the exact location of the anchor before it was covered up again by the sand. We had attached several markers, but they were removed by souvenir seekers, or perhaps by people who were determined to keep the anchor in its resting place beneath the sand. Greg assured the group that, with his careful measurements, we would be able to find the anchor.

George Powell told us he could assist in a more scientific way. He had a heavy duty metal detector that would be able to find the anchor more precisely. He would bring it with him on Tuesday to locate the anchor before we begin to dig.

*   *   *   *   *

It was a beautiful day on Tuesday, September 20, 1983 when Greg, Jonathan and I arrived on the beach, earlier than the appointed twelve o'clock noon hour. I could feel the warmth of the September sun as it warmed the surface of my skin, and was grateful for the slight ocean breeze that would keep us cool as we performed the tasks that lie ahead. I walked down to the water to test the temperature; it felt pleasantly warm.

It was about halfway to low tide by now, and, just as predicted by the autumnal equinox, in a short while the tide would be dead low. While I had a few moments to myself, I searched the beach, just one more time, looking for another piece of tile from the *Fortuna*, thinking that it would set a nice mood for the anchor's excavation if I found one. But the sea did not cooperate, and I did not find another tile or any reminder that the *Fortuna* was still with us on the beach.

The tide receded rapidly and as the recovery crew began to arrive, we paced off the route leading to the anchor, following Greg's precisely calculated directions. One, two, three-- eighteen, nineteen, etc. As we approached the end of the path, something caught my eye. And as surely as I am writing this part of the story, for a brief moment, my heart stopped beating.

"Look at that, Greg. Look right here!" I yelled in excitement."Exactly where you said the anchor would be. There's a tiny piece of the yellow cord we put on the anchor to mark the spot. It's barely poking through the sand. What a lucky break," I said, reassured that we would be digging in the right place. But, was it luck, or fate, or divine intervention that, again, gave me a sign? I didn't question the source; I was just thankful for the answer.

"It's down there all right," Greg stated reassuringly.

When the crew arrived and learned the anchor had been located and was within our reach, they were eager to begin the recovery. First to arrive was George Powell, dressed in his usual tan work clothes, triumphantly driving a bright yellow front loader across the beach to the site of the buried anchor. He was going to use his front loader to gobble up the sand from around the anchor, hoping to quickly expose a good portion of it. Mayor Nissen, by now known to everyone as Bob, and Jan were the next to arrive, along with several firemen and interested townspeople. A crowd of roughly fifty to seventy five people soon gathered. Bob walked down the beach to meet us at the edge of the water, and for the first time ever during this whole project asked, "Okay, where's the anchor?" When we pointed to the tiny yellow cord that was poking through the sand, his face was swallowed by a huge grin as he turned to face the crowd and encouragingly yelled, "Let's go get it!"

The firemen hooked their hoses to the nearby hydrant on 16th Street, stretching them over the dune to the site of the buried anchor. A rather large man with a full beard, dressed in work clothes crossed over the dune and blended himself in with the crowd. I remember asking Jan who he was, and he merely responded that he was "nobody."

Within minutes we could hear the faint chug-chug-chug of what sounded like a locomotive approaching its station. It was quite a spectacular sight to see Paul Buterick maneuvering his tall orange crane through the narrow passageway onto the beach.

Paul was a youthful looking man, clearly capable of handling the task assigned to him - and then some. Judging from the muscles he had developed while working at Buterick Bulkheading, his family owned business, it was obvious that he did an awful lot of the manual labor himself. His deep golden tan was no doubt obtained through hours of working outdoors. He looked like a movie star. And, to the casual observer, the activity on the beach could very well have been a movie set.

The crowd continued to grow, and we could hear their words of encouragement above the loud puttering noise of the big crane. In no time at all, the crane was in position near the tiny piece of yellow rope that marked the anchor's location. Hoses were attached to three fire engines to pump water to the crane's rail that would be used to jet the sand from around the anchor. The jet had a two-inch nozzle that would be lowered down into the pool to do its work. Paul's stern warning "under no circumstances should anyone get their foot under the jet because it would leave nothing but bones in a fraction of a second" painted a clear picture of its power. It was like running a knife through soft butter; the pressure of the water just ate away at the sand until it left a large hole in its place. After a few minutes of jetting the water down the rail and into the sand where the anchor was located, the once clear water began to change color. It turned rusty brown, which could only mean one thing: "We've hit it," Paul called out to his crew. "We've hit the anchor."

The hole quickly filled, creating a pool of water colored a deep brown from the rust of the *Fortuna's* anchor. I never thought I'd be so happy to see the ocean's water look so dirty. Without fanfare, the unknown man with a beard, dressed in his work clothes, eased his way out of the crowd and up to the edge of the pool. His name was William Sylvester, and though unknown to Jan Nissen, he was no stranger to the others. He was a volunteer fireman, and like most people who volunteer, came prepared to help. William had grown up with his family in Ship Bottom; lived there all his life, he said proudly. He was certain that his mother would have seen the *Fortuna* wreck, and he was going to help get the anchor out, "just for her." Quickly removing his jacket, hat and boots, William then jumped into the water to help locate the anchor below. He swam around the pool like a fish, often disappearing beneath the rusty water then surfacing with a grin.

"It's there. I felt it," he yelled as the crowd cheered. "It's the part with the ball on it."

Paul directed, "Let's see if we can hook the chain around it and see if it's ready to lift out." Paul and William took turns diving into the brown water to secure the chain, each time coming up without success. The chain's hook kept slipping off. There was no easy way to do it. Somebody had to dive down and go under the anchor to secure the chain around the stock. It was a really dangerous thing to do. If at any time the water jet stopped pumping, the sand slurry could settle so quickly that he might get trapped under tons of wet sand; as if he were buried in cement. In Paul's mind, there was little doubt about whose job it was going to be. He was the one who said he would get the anchor out, and knowing the dangers of going into the water with the jet stream swirling the sand around, he felt that he owned the responsibility. He disappeared beneath the surface of the water but quickly resurfaced for a breath of air. There was a slight problem with his plan; he was too buoyant to stay submerged long enough to complete the job. He needed someone to hold him under while he looped the chain under the arm of the anchor. He motioned for Greg to come in the water and stand on his shoulders to hold him down, but Greg knew of the dangers involved and told him, no, he shouldn't try it. Paul was more than insistent, and after putting a "safety signal" in place, Greg stood on his shoulders as he disappeared beneath the water for another try. Just as the crowd began to worry that he had been under the water a little longer than they thought he should have been, Greg swam aside as Paul broke through the smooth surface of the water like a shooting star and triumphantly motioned "thumbs up."

"It's attached. The anchor is attached to the crane, ready to be lifted," Paul stated in a voice of modest accomplishment. His hair was coated with fine sand, blasted there by the jet action of the fire hose and his skin had been scratched by the sharp particles of sand that flew through the turbulent water like tiny razors. But he didn't seem to mind. His mission had been accomplished. The chain was secured to the anchor, and the anchor was within reach.

As the fire truck began to jet the water into the pool to remove the last bit of sand from around the anchor, a connector broke and the hose shot into the air, reeling wildly like an untamed snake. It flung around, throwing a violent stream of water in every direction. The crowd retreated, giving the hose all the room it needed as the firemen recovered it and turned it off. The hose now lay motionless on the sand, having lost its power and usefulness.

Though this setback was a disappointment, it could not have come at a better time. The incoming tide had shortened the beach, limiting the area in which we could work. The day was "called on of account of incoming tide." We'd hoped to recover the anchor in just one day, and had the hose not failed, perhaps we could have. The good news was we had located the anchor and knew it was within reach; it could not elude us now. We would come back to finish the job tomorrow. One end of the chain was left attached to the anchor; the other end was removed from the crane. The crew then packed up the crane and reversed its direction up over the dune and off the beach. The fire trucks returned to the station, and the work crew went home to rest up for another try tomorrow.

But when tomorrow came, the weather was uncooperative. The wind was so strong it made another attempt impossible. The forecast was better for Friday, so Friday it would be. During the two day hiatus, Paul came up with another plan, still determined to "come back every day if I have to until I get that anchor out."

And determined he was. Friday was a beautiful Long Beach Island beach day: sunny with only a slight, cooling breeze. A crowd of interested spectators and members of the media started to gather on the beach in hopes of witnessing this historic event. At twelve o'clock sharp, Paul crested the dune driving a tall orange rig with the manufacturer's name "AMERICAN" written in large black letters across the back. It was a nice touch. Norman Rockwell could not have painted a better scene. Paul unhooked the crane from the flat bed that carried it from the mainland earlier in the day and drove it onto the beach to the recovery site. He also brought a clam-shell digger to attach to the front of the crane. With jaws as big as a giant dinosaur's, it would remove the sand in minutes instead of hours.

The incoming tide had nearly filled the hole with sand. Paul's crew attached the clam shell digger to the end of the crane and it quickly ate away the sand, forming a fresh, new pool. The tide was a little higher than it was on the day of our first attempt; much higher than we had anticipated. George Powell brought 100 burlap bags for us to fill with sand so we could make a dam around the pool to hold back the incoming tide. As if on cue, several people stepped forward from the crowd and grabbed shovels to help fill the sand bags. Once filled, the bags were carefully placed at the water's edge to form a wall around the recovery site. It was a very good plan, and it worked perfectly.

Paul started the motor on the crane to begin the recovery operation. The water in the pool was still, and the crowd remained silent as the crane prepared to hoist the anchor from beneath the water. The crane heaved forward, trying to raise the heavy, invisible object. But not a single ripple appeared on the water's surface. The anchor did not budge. They gave it a few more tries but still the anchor refused to leave its grave of seventy three years.

"We need to determine its exact position," requested Paul as he searched the workers for a volunteer to brave the depth of the murky pool. But no one stepped forward to accept the assignment. "I have to get some kind of bearing on how it's positioned so I'll know in what direction to nudge her."

"Well," I said to myself. "This was my project from the first time I uttered the words 'I think we can get the anchor out', so it is up to me to stand behind my project one hundred and ten percent. Someone has to go into the water to find out how the anchor is resting. That someone has to be me."

Appropriately dressed in my "Ask Me About the Anchor" t-shirt, I put on my sneakers to protect my feet from any sharp rusty protrusions that I might encounter and edged my way into the pool. I had no sooner entered the water when I realized I had company.

"Well, you're not going to have to do this alone," said William. "You go down on this side, and I'll try the other. Try to feel it with your feet first."

I slowly walked along the stock of the anchor like a tightrope walker, carefully balancing myself as I stepped. The anchor was in the perfect position. It was nearly straight up. By measuring it with my feet, I could judge it to be about four or five feet before hitting the shank where the chain had been secured. I dove under the water to make sure the chain was still attached. While I was under the water I used my hands to feel my way around the anchor, caressing the large shackle that was once used to hoist the anchor a long time ago. I felt so connected to the anchor; I didn't want to let go. I completed my inspection and then surfaced. The expression on my face gave it away before I could motion "thumbs up."

"The chain is right around the stock, and it's well secured. Feels like it's standing pretty straight up," I shouted to Paul. He was delighted with my report.

William, who also inspected the anchor with his feet and hands as we groped around the water in a playful-looking scene, agreed. "She's ready when you are." We exited the water, shivering from the chill of the late afternoon breeze.

The sounds of the crane were deafening as it strained to make another pull. It leaned so far forward I was afraid it might tip over. Operating the crane with the hands of a skilled surgeon, Paul gave a few jerky tugs that rocked the submerged anchor back and forth beneath the water. Then suddenly, the suction that held it in place for so long broke loose. Giant ripples appeared on the water as the anchor was partially lifted out of the pool. The crowd gasped and cheered as they viewed the *Fortuna's* anchor for the very first time. Inch by inch the anchor was raised until it was about half way out of the water. Suddenly, Paul turned off the motor on the crane and, holding the anchor in place as if frozen in time, called out in a booming voice, "I think it's the wrong one. I'll have to put it back."

A loud roar escaped from the crowd as we cheered and hollered to convince Paul that this was the one we wanted, so go ahead and get it out! He restarted the motor on the crane and continued to lift the anchor until it was free from the sand, hanging magnificently in the air above the speechless crowd.

It was 3:44 p.m. The tide was starting to breech the wall of sandbags, letting us know we had completed the job just before our time ran out.

My feelings of elation are hard to describe. The anchor was truly a beauty. And, most importantly, my biggest fear was relieved; the anchor was complete. At a whopping 10 feet x 10 feet 2 inches x 7 feet fluke to fluke, it was larger than most of us expected by a foot in both directions. The claim plate we affixed in May, claiming it for the town of Ship Bottom, was still attached and as legible as the day it was made. The anchor was encrusted with shells, fishing lures, pieces of the wire rigging from the ship, red pieces of tile and small, slug-like pieces of metal. It was beautiful! While the anchor was resting on the beach at the edge of the water, Bob Nissen, with a hammer and chisel in hand, quietly approached the anchor and began chipping away at the encrustations. Moments later he presented me with the prize: a whole tile - one that was placed as ballast on the *Fortuna* in 1909. It had been nestled in the crotch of the anchor between the two large flukes. I was both excited to finally have a whole tile and so touched by his thoughtful gesture that I broke into tears. I never gave him five dollars.

The anchor was carefully loaded onto a flatbed for transport to Bob Nissen's marine shop just a few blocks away, with strict instructions from Paul: "don't drop it."

As crowds of excited spectators gathered around the anchor inspecting every glorious inch of it, Paul and his crew worked tirelessly in the background to restore the beach to its "pre-anchor recovery" condition. By the time his crew left, there were no visible signs of the events that had taken place on the beach that day.

The *Fortuna's* anchor had been a newsworthy story on Long Beach Island, and one the media had followed from the very beginning. Immediately after it was extracted from the sand and press photos were taken, the anchor became old news. The newspaper reporters then focused their attention on me, who now had rightfully earned the title "The Anchor Lady."

"Well, Carole, now that the anchor is out, what are your feelings about it?" asked a reporter.

"I'm excited to finally see it. But right now? I'm still a bit numb from the experience," I responded. "To tell you the truth, I'm almost, but not entirely, speechless. You can't even imagine how relieved I am that the anchor is whole. My biggest fear was that there would only be a piece of it. Not the whole anchor. I thought it might be tangled up in the remaining pieces of the wreck and we couldn't get it free."

Then suddenly, thrusting a microphone in my face, the reporter asked, "Now that you have the anchor out, what are you going to do next?"

I didn't know what to say, and I don't really know where the words came from, but I answered his question without hesitation. "Well, I guess the next thing would be to find the newborn baby who was rescued from the *Fortuna* in 1910." I'm not sure why I said that. Did I speak too soon or had it already been a plan held in my subconscious? Thoughts began to swirl through my mind. The baby. How on earth does one find a baby without a name, or date of birth? Without knowing where it lives, or if that person was even still living? Right then and there I told all the Southern New Jersey newspaper subscribers that I'd find the *Fortuna* baby. Oh, my. Where do I start?

Immediately, I realized I needed more information in order to begin my search for the baby. Some information obtained from Lloyd's Registry would help: Captain's name: G.B. Adragna, and Owner: B. Savona. It was at least a place to start.

When I was in eighth grade, we took a class trip to Washington D.C., and I remember feeling dwarfed, standing in front of the National Archives building. I recalled being told that all important records are housed within that building; surely a record of the *Fortuna* shipwreck might be important enough to be on file. I wrote to the National Archives and Records Service asking just that: do you have a manifest of those aboard the Fortuna? The name of the ship's captain was G.B. Adragna, and was owned by B. Savona. Do you also have, or know where I can obtain, an accounting of the ship's loss? I'm certain it was a news item back then and a report of it must be available somewhere.

Their reply was all I needed to begin my search for the baby. For a $5.00 fee, they mailed me copies of all three wreck reports filed by the U.S. Life Saving Services that participated in the rescue operations of the *Fortuna* in 1910. It was the best $5.00 I ever spent!

The clamshell digger removes sand from around the anchor.

The anchor is intact after being buried for 73 years.

The Fortuna anchor has been recovered.

Buterick Bulkheading's crane gets ready to recover anchor.

Paul Buterick with recovered anchor at monument site.

Riches do not consist in the possession of treasures but in the use made of them.

Napoleon Bonaparte

Spring - 1984

Everyone agreed: the anchor was a precious jewel that needed to have a proper setting. I had a few thoughts of my own on how to display the anchor and discussed them with Mayor Nissen, but the final decision was ultimately up to him and his Council. My thought was it should go on the front lawn of the Ship Bottom Borough Hall so that everyone can learn something about its history. I was pleased that he shared the same thought. Was it just a coincidence that the Borough Hall was located down the street from where the *Fortuna* left her anchor behind seventy three years before?

*   *   *   *   *

I'd met her in the Hand's Store in Ship Bottom while doing a little early morning shopping. I didn't know who she was, but she must have recognized me from a photo published in the local newspaper. She introduced herself as she approached. "I'm Linda Feaster, with the Ship Bottom Civic Association." She continued to tell me how great it was that I was going to preserve the *Fortuna* anchor for the town, and that she wished more people had the insight to do things like that. She told me the Civic Association is always looking for projects and if I needed any help with fundraising, I should get in touch with them. She'd wished me luck then we parted, each going our separate ways.

I knew I needed help with this project and was very grateful for Linda's offer. Being only a summer resident, I was not at all familiar with the way things like this worked on the Island. And, fundraising? That certainly was not my forté. I wrote a letter to the Civic Association, offering to give a history of the *Fortuna* at one of their meetings. I wanted to explain why it was desirable for Ship Bottom to support the construction of a monument, and ask for help in raising the money to build it. The Association responded they were "in- between projects and were looking for something positive to do for Ship Bottom." My offer was gratefully accepted, and I was invited to speak at their February meeting.

I was introduced to the Association as *The Anchor Lady* and told the story of the *Fortuna*, one some knew briefly and some not at all. Instantly, they fell in love with the project. I presented a list of objectives, dividing the project into three phases: essential, desirable, and dream. The essentials included preservation, documentation and construction of the anchor monument. Desirables included exhibition materials. And the dream was a plane ticket to fly "the baby," if located, to Ship Bottom for the dedication ceremony of the *Fortuna's* anchor. As far as the essential and desirable items were concerned, the members unanimously supported them. But a plane ticket for the baby? Many thought I'd never locate it. Others thought it would cost too much. That part of the plan would be put on hold until later, if and when the baby was found.

Meanwhile, in the back of the room, wheels were turning in the mind of one particular member of the association. John Carpenter, a licensed architect who spent summers with his family in Ship Bottom, had not planned on going to the meeting that night. But he was down for the weekend and didn't have any plans for the evening. He decided to attend the meeting, just to see what was going on. During my presentation, I asked for ideas on how to display the anchor; John was already busy, sketching out a plan. At the end of the meeting, in his usual, shy, quiet, manner, he presented me with his sketch of a proposed monument and promised a finished drawing in time for the next meeting. Later I learned, though not from John, that he was the architect who designed the addition to the borough hall building. Not only was he familiar with Ship Bottom's building codes, but he would be sure to create a design that would enhance *his* building. We could not have asked for a more qualified candidate to design the anchor's new home.

At the March meeting John produced, as promised, a complete set of blueprints for construction of the monument. He wowed the group with his hand-made scale model of the monument to allow those who could not imagine beyond the printed paper to see what the finished display would look like. It was very impressive. Now all we needed was the money to build it.

It was at the end of the meeting when I met Eleanor Smith, a self-proclaimed Long Beach Island historian (and rightfully so). Long Beach Island is not a very big place, so it was only a matter of time before our paths would cross. As Eleanor approached me with deep frown lines showing in her forehead, she addressed me in a scolding tone of voice. "Oh, so you're Carole Bradshaw?" Acknowledging that indeed I was, she continued. "I live in Ship Bottom; I have for a really long time. Over the years, I had collected so many of those red tiles of yours that I had them set into the hearth of my fireplace. Every time someone would ask me where they came from I didn't have an answer because I didn't know. Nobody did. All I knew was that I collected them on the beach. So, I made up the story that when Thomas Jefferson was building Monticello, he ordered the tiles from France, and when the ship that carried them wrecked on our beach, I got them instead of Thomas Jefferson! It really did make an interesting story, and then you came along and poked a big hole in my tale. Now, I still tell the Thomas Jefferson story, but I do give you the credit for finding the real history of those tiles." I laughed at her story, admitting that I found it to be a little more exciting than the truth. I asked her if I could tell her story in my future presentations, and she didn't hesitate a moment before answering "gladly."

Enthusiasm and support for the anchor project spread rapidly through the town. Many people offered ideas on how to raise money to construct the monument. The T-Shirt suggestion won, hands down. It was the early 1980's and at that time, the best way to get your message out to the people was to print it on a T-shirt. If you wanted people to eat at your pizza place, advertise on a shirt. If you loved your dog, say it on a T-shirt. People of all shapes, sizes and ages wore T-shirts, and people paid attention to the message printed on them. Rick Bourgeois, the head artist at *Starving Artist*, a specialty T-shirt shop on the Island, offered to design a shirt for us. His initial design depicting the anchor resting on top of the shield-shaped pad, surrounded by the words "FORTUNA" and "SHIP BOTTOM" was almost perfect. Being a real perfectionist, he was all set to straighten out the bend in the anchor, thinking it got bent when someone dropped it. I pointed out that it was supposed to have a bend and followed with a two minute history of the design of anchors. 'It was around 1850 that someone discovered if the shorter arm of the sand anchor were to be bent, it would set better in use providing better anchorage to the ship. Probably a German who thought of it because sand anchors were the design of German craftsmen.' Rick took note and finished his design. The shirts were printed historically correct with the bent arm of the anchor. The initial run of two hundred shirts sold out in less than two weeks. It was quite a sight to see *Fortuna* shirts being worn by hundreds of people all over the Island. And so it was that the *Fortuna* shirt became *the* T-shirt of 1984. We were successfully spreading the word, and interest in the *Fortuna* and our treasury began to grow. But the treasury did not grow fast enough. We brainstormed other ideas and came up with one that would become a permanent part of the monument.

John Carpenter's design featured a shield-shaped pad where the anchor would rest, surrounded by fifteen posts with a chain threaded through holes bored in the top. The posts added a finished look to the monument, and quartered off the area to keep trespassers out. We came up with the idea of attaching engraved brass plaques to the posts. People could purchase them in the name of their family, in memory of a special person, or with a personal message of their own. Through the advertising efforts of the Ship Bottom Civic Association, the sale of the plaques took off right from the start. Hundreds of people purchased them so they could become a part of the monument. That was all we needed to earn the full amount of money needed to build the monument. The leftover money would be held in trust for future maintenance. The head post would honor Captain Adragna, his family and crew, along with information about the wreck. All other posts were quickly filled with the purchased plaques.

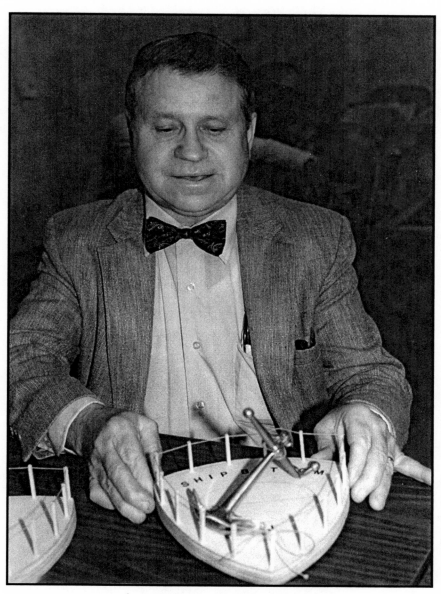

Architect John Carpenter with model of
his Fortuna monument design

John Guld trowels cement base of anchor monument.

1869-1910

Mosaic tiles depict beached Fortuna on monument base.

Let no one ever come to you without leaving better and happier.

Mother Theresa

Spring / Summer - 1984

I reached across my paper-strewn desk, picked up the telephone and timidly dialed the number for the United Nations. "Good Morning. Italian Consulate." The voice on the other end of the phone spoke with such a thick, heavy accent it was nearly impossible to understand her words.

"Excuse me?" I questioned. "Have I reached the Italian Consulate?"

She kindly repeated her greeting, "Italian Consulate." Surely they could offer the help I needed to find the *Fortuna* baby. I identified myself and condensed my request to a simple "I am trying to contact a family descendent living in Sicily. A telephone directory of Trapani would be a big help. Would you have one available?" Simple. Concise. And to the point. "I won't need the entire book," I continued; "just the "A" pages which include the family name ADRAGNA."

"Wait one moment, please. I will check for you." After a pause which seemed like half a lifetime, the woman returned to the phone with her reply. "Yes, I do have a listing for ADRAGNA in Trapani. Would you like me to send you a Photostat copy?"

"Yes, I would appreciate that very much," I graciously thanked her. I could feel my heart racing a mile a minute. I wanted to jump up and down and tell everyone in sight how I was going to locate the missing baby but there was no one around to tell. Instead, I calmly finished giving my address to the woman at the Consulate, asking if she could please mail it right away. I never did get her name, but she assured me that she would send the pages to me as soon as possible.

Immediately I started counting the days the mailman came and went by without even as much as a bill or throw-away newspaper circular. Nothing. One day stretched into two, then three, four and five, with still no mail from the Consulate. Had the woman forgotten about my request entirely? Maybe she just felt they weren't in the business of finding missing persons. When ten days passed and still no envelope, my hopes turned into disappointment and I stopped rushing to the mailbox when the delivery truck came. Maybe it was time to think of another way to contact the Adragna families in Trapani.

It was a little over two weeks when the envelope from the Consulate finally arrived. I stood at the mailbox for a moment, staring at the large manila envelope, teasingly resting on the top of the stack of letters. I gathered the bundle of mail, walked into the house and closed the door behind me. I sat down at the kitchen table and, staring at the envelope, wondered if it was bringing good news or disappointment. There was only one way to find out. I drew a deep breath, tore open the seal, spilling the contents of the envelope on the table. Two pages of names! There were over a hundred *Adragnas* listed in Trapani. With postage costing forty-four cents per letter, I knew I had to do some careful elimination. I had no idea whether the baby I was looking for was male or female but I thought if the baby were a male he might bear the same first name as his father. But there was no *G.B.*, or even a *G.* or a *B. Adragna* listed. And, if the baby were a girl, she would probably have married and changed her name. I made the decision to send letters only to the male *Adragnas*, all seventy three of them.

I knew I would need some expert assistance for this part of the project, so I drafted my letter:

March 10, 1984

Dear Sir,

I am doing research on the maritime disasters along the Coast of Long Beach Island, New Jersey, USA, and I am looking for information pertaining to the *Fortuna* which sailed from the Port of Trapani as long ago as 1909. I have the following information:

Ship: *Fortuna* - Signal letters PHGT
Owned by: B. Savona
Bound for New York via Montevideo and Barbados
Sank in Ship Bottom, Long Beach Island,
New Jersey USA January 18, 1910

Captain of *Fortuna*: G.B. Adragna

A rescue attempt was made by the Ship Bottom Lifesaving Station, which rescued all aboard (13 crew members, Captain, his wife and three children) but the boat could not be saved and was sold for salvage. All crew members were given passage to New York on January 25, 1910 and it was assumed they went home to Trapani.

I'm trying to locate an ancestor of Captain Adragna. On board the *Fortuna* were his three children, one a newly born baby, born after the ship left Trapani in 1909. I do not know if children were male or female; only that there were three. I would appreciate any help you can give me in locating any of these children. I would like to write or contact them to share the many photographs and information I have regarding their father's ship.

Thank you for any information you can give me, and for the time and inconvenience it may have caused you. It is important for my research project that I have this information as soon as you can find any. Your efforts are greatly appreciated.

Sincerely,
Franco Di Gangi

Franco Di Gangi! You are probably wondering who is Franco Di Gangi? By the sound of his name, you might already have guessed he is Italian. Actually, he was born in Sicily, but at a very young age moved to Rome where he spent the greater part of his youth. Though he has been in America since the early 1950s, his thick accent still gives overt clues to his heritage. Often when he struggles to express a thought in English he just gives up, laughs at himself and reverts to his native Italian tongue.

Franco is one of two barbers, both Italian, in our little town of Caldwell, New Jersey. It was during the time right after I found the anchor that my five year old son, Jonathan, needed a haircut. I've always enjoyed chatting with Franco while he snipped away on Jonathan's hair; his topics of conversation were so colorful. He always had something interesting to share, and he told his stories like a theatrical performer. While Jonathan was being seated on a booster seat made of folded towels, I asked Franco for a favor.

"Franco, you still speak Italian, don't you?" I asked.

"Oh, sure," was his short reply." What do you need?"

I told him that I was looking for a family, actually one person in particular, who lived in Trapani in Sicily. When he asked if it was a relative that I was looking for, I told him the story, starting with "I found an anchor from a ship that wrecked in 1910," and ending with "and rescued from the ship was a newborn baby." I explained that I was searching for that baby who I think might have returned to Trapani. I showed him the letter I planned to send to the Adragnas listed in the Trapani phone directory. He agreed it would be more effective if the letter were written in and signed by an Italian.

"Since I don't know Italian, would you translate it for me?" I asked.

"Oh, sure. You know I will be happy to. Tell me, this sounds very interesting. Do you know anything about the baby?" Franco asked as he continued to clip Jonathan's hair.

I admitted that I did not know much, only that the baby was a newborn, and it was born to the captain's wife while on board the *Fortuna*. I didn't even know if it was a boy or a girl, or if they actually returned to Sicily after the shipwreck. By this time, Franco was hooked on the story, and I was reeling him in.

He agreed that while this was a good place to start, the same letter should also be sent to the mayor of Trapani. And, most of all, one should go to the Harbormaster since he would have an intimate knowledge of everything that went on in the harbor and the name might just ring a bell to him. (Jonathan received a very nice haircut that day, and Franco's tip was more generous than usual.)

Franco translated the letter, but at the same time cautioned me not to be too disappointed if I didn't get a response. "Sometimes," he said, "the Italian people, well, they are not too anxious to help out."

Seventy-three air mail letters! Do you have any idea what a stack of seventy three letters looks like? It looks impressive. But for a $35 investment in postage and paper, if just one person responded, the effort would be worth every penny spent.

I mailed the letters in early June, hoping for a reply in about two weeks. None came. The school season had just ended and, as usual, we packed up our belongings and headed back to our summer house on Long Beach Island. This summer would be different than previous ones when my days were centered on carefree beach activities; there was still a lot of work to be done on the anchor. It had been stored in Bob Nissen's boat garage over the winter while we searched for the proper coating to preserve it. Soon the anchor would be moved to my driveway so I could clean it and apply a coating of the preservative recommended by the Smithsonian Institute. It was going to be a busy summer.

One of the most time consuming - and I must admit, enjoyable - of my summer activities would be traveling the local "lecture circuit" to spread the word about the *Fortuna*. After each presentation, I was always amazed to find someone in the audience who knew someone who participated in the rescue, or could add something new to the story. One time, as I was telling the story of the shipwreck, a gasp came from somewhere in the audience when I mentioned the name of the *Fortuna's* captain, Giovan Adragna. At the end of my presentation when I opened the floor to questions and discussion, the man who let out the gasp stood up and, to my surprise, remarked, "My name is Joseph [Giuseppe in Italian] Adragna. You can imagine how shocked I was to hear you tell about my family name. I have been trying to research my family in Italy, and this might just be the branch I have been unable to find."

If you think he was shocked, you can imagine how I felt. Had I been researching the family the hard way, when right here in a town next to Long Beach Island lived a man with the captain's name? And, he speaks English! Who would have thought there would be an Adragna living about two miles from where Captain Adragna's ship wrecked, and he would be attending my presentation? Certainly not I. Small world. I wondered if he was related to "my" Captain Adragna, but further research determined that his family was in no way connected to the *Fortuna* Adragnas.

My anchor presentations were gaining in popularity, and I soon found myself giving as many as three a week. Not only was the honorarium boosting the anchor fund's treasury, but I was out spreading the word and people were listening. I no longer had to depend on my "Hi, I'm Carole Bradshaw. Ask Me About the Anchor" T-shirt to publicize the project. My children, who often walked several feet behind me when I wore it through the streets of Long Beach Island, were glad when I no longer played the role of a walking billboard. I didn't give up on my shirt completely; I adopted it as my official "uniform" for my anchor presentations.

It was early July when the mailman delivered a letter forwarded from our permanent residence in Caldwell. We don't get much mail delivered to our beach address during the summer because most of it is not forwarded. When something was delivered, there was always a mad dash to the mailbox to see who the lucky recipients were. Today it was my lucky day; it was a letter from Franco. By this time I had just about forgotten that we were once anxiously awaiting a reply from Sicily. I opened the letter and was greeted by the large, hand-written words: "WE DID IT!"

Inside the envelope was a letter written in Italian which had been graciously translated by Franco. The letter was from the mayor of Trapani, saying he had located the family of Captain Giovan Adragna. The letter stated (translation): 22 June 1984: Captain Adragna Giovan Battista of Giuseppe (his father) and of Antonina (his mother) born in Trapani January 1, 1867 and passed away in Trapani June 3, 1954. Adragna Giuseppe (son of Captain Adragna) born May 4, 1912 and living in Trapani at Via Delle Acacie No. 27. Signed: il Sindaco.

In my excitement, I read the letter too fast and took this for the second greatest news in the anchor project, second only to finding the anchor, of course. We found the baby! We found the baby! I was so thrilled and couldn't wait to share my news. I called Greg at work and told him I found the baby. My news caught him completely off guard, and he wondered aloud what in the world I was talking about.

"The *Fortuna* baby. I found the *Fortuna* baby," I kept saying over and over again. "I just got a letter from Franco. He received a letter from the mayor of Trapani. Here, I'll read it to you. Giuseppe, son of

Giovan Battista Adragna, Captain, and Maria Savona Adragna, born on May 4, 1912."

"Wait a minute, read that again, will you?" Greg asked.

"Giuseppe, son of Giovan Battista Adragna, Captain, and Maria Savona Adragna, born on May 4, 1912. 1912? 1912! Oh. If he was born in 1912, then he can't be the baby born on the *Fortuna* in 1909."

I was so disappointed. He was not the baby I was looking for after all. But, this baby was born two years after the *Fortuna* wrecked on the shores of Long Beach Island; two years after the captain was supposed to have committed suicide after losing his ship. If I could prove that this was really Captain Adragna's son, then I could prove the captain's death was not an indirect result of the *Fortuna's* wreck. I was now more excited than ever. Even though I hadn't found the baby born on the *Fortuna*, I knew I was getting closer. As an added bonus, I might have inadvertently corrected an error in the recorded history of the *Fortuna*.

My excitement over finding a descendant of Captain Adragna was interrupted by a phone call early Monday morning.

"Hello. My name is Joseph Previto. I would like to explain to you why I am calling," said the voice on the other end of the phone. His voice sounded stern; his tone, direct. "It is in regards to the letter you sent to the Adragna families in Sicily. I was visiting with Giuseppe Adragna and he showed me the letter Franco wrote to the mayor of Trapani, requesting information about their family. I called Franco Di Gangi, and he immediately told me it was your project and I should get in touch with you. Can you tell me more about this project and why it is so important that you contact someone of the family?"

What have I done now was my first thought. Early on in my research someone had warned me to be careful, that I had no way of knowing what I was getting myself into. I brushed it off thinking he had just seen too many movies! Now, I wasn't so sure. I'd purposely kept the information in my letter vague, mentioning only that I was trying to locate the baby born on the *Fortuna*. I said nothing about finding the anchor and our plans for a big dedication celebration. This lack of detail bothered Joseph Previto. He assured the Adragnas he would check me out when he returned to the States, and if everything seemed to be on the up and up, he would then give them the go ahead to write back to me. I told Joe the pertinent details: the anchor, the remains of the ship still buried on the beach, the plans for a dedication ceremony, and if the money could be raised, to bring the baby back to America for the dedication. He seemed pleased with the story; he even became a bit emotional. After a moment or two of silence, Joe admitted he was getting only good vibes about the story, but he still found it hard to believe I was doing all this just because I thought it was a nice thing to do. He thought most people would have a motive; maybe money, position, fame? But just to do it because it was good seemed un-natural to him. To me it was the most logical plan: find something, do something good with it, and include as many people who would benefit.

Joe said he would let the Adragnas know it would be all right to contact me; that my intentions are good, and they could satisfy my wishes. I thanked him for his kind intervention on behalf of the Adragna family, and assured him that I had no hidden agenda for this project. I would be doing exactly what I said I would, and nothing more. I promised to keep in touch, and he did, likewise.

Several weeks after my conversation with Joseph Previto, I received another letter from Franco with a translation of Giuseppe's letter included:

August 6, 1984

Dear Mr. Di Gangi,

I thank you very much for the idea to erect a monument to my father. He saved the crew and his own family when the *Fortuna* sank in Long Beach Island.

We are very happy and proud that your initiative will culminate in erecting a monument to my father and we wish that we could be present.

My father was born in Trapani the 1st of January 1867, and died in Trapani 3 June 1954. His wife was Savona Maria and they had four children.

1. Adragna, Antonina - deceased
2. Adragna, Anna - deceased

3. Adragna, Saveria Fortunata Marina - Born in Barbados 25 November 1909 - living
4. Adragna, Giuseppe - born in Trapani 4 May 1912 - living

So as you can see the daughter, Saveria, was born during the trip and when the ship sank (January 1910) she was about one month and a half. Since we were so young we do not remember much, but we can say that my father as a captain was a very good one and that he worked for many companies.

In order to prove to you that we are the children, I will send to you, in the next letter, the following:

(1) a photo of my father
(2) a family photo with my father
(3) a photo of myself
(4) a photo of Saveria (born on the ship)
(5) a photo of the *Fortuna*

I wish you will send us a copy of the story of the boat *Fortuna* and all about the reason of its sinking and of whatever you know. We children appreciate very much what you are doing about the memory of my father and we thank you very, very much.

God Bless you.

Adragna Giuseppe
Adragna Saveria Fortunata Marina

This time it was for real. At long last, I had found the *Fortuna* baby. My excitement was unimaginable. And, they would be sending photos so I could see what they looked like! When I first started my fascination with the *Fortuna*, I had created an image of Captain Adragna in my mind, and I was anxious to see if he compared to it. It was hard to just sit back and wait. Patience is not one of my virtues.

When the photographs Giuseppe promised arrived, I'd be willing to bet my screams of excitement were heard clear across the ocean to Sicily! Never in my wildest dreams had I imagined that Captain Adragna would look, well, like that! He was such a handsome man, tall in stature, dressed in all the fineries of an aristocrat. He had dark hair and a full moustache. A likeness to Tom Selleck immediately came to mind. In the photograph, taken in 1916, he was surrounded by his beautiful family: his wife Maria; the two daughters who sailed on the *Fortuna's* last voyage, Antonina 13, and Anna 10; Saveria, the baby born on the ship, 7, and their only son, Giuseppe, 5.

*   *   *   *   *

I received my first letter from Saveria on September 6, 1984. In her letter, she explained the painful emotions she felt when the mayor of Trapani showed up at her apartment. The first thing he asked her was "are you the daughter of Captain Giovan Adragna; the one who was born on board the *Fortuna*?" She didn't know why, after all these years, he wanted to know. And she was afraid to answer him. Of course *she* knew she was born on board the *Fortuna* on the Island of Barbados in the Netherland Antilles. But how did he know that? (The *Fortuna* and both her parents were Italian, which automatically gave Saveria Italian citizenship, but her official birth records were filed after they returned home, and they show that she was born in Rome in 1912.) She gathered her courage, and still shaking when she answered, truthfully stated that, yes, she was born on the *Fortuna*. With trembling hands, she took the letter the mayor had received from Franco Di Gangi and went back inside her apartment to share the experience with Giuseppe.

Giuseppe read the letter the mayor gave to Saveria in which Franco wrote that he was trying to locate the baby born on the *Fortuna*. But the reasons why he wanted to find the baby were unclear. Why, after so many years, was someone interested in their father's ship? They thought the United States government might make them pay to remove some remaining parts of the wreckage from the beach. Saveria and Giuseppe both decided to wait and give it more thought before responding to Franco Di Gangi. But, the more they thought about it, the less worried and more curious they became. They needed to find out what all the interest in the *Fortuna* was about.

Franco Di Gangi spent many enjoyable hours translating my English words to Saveria into Italian. As she wrote back, Franco would translate her words into English. Saveria always wrote as if she were speaking directly to me, without the thought of going through a translator. I felt certain Franco embellished my letters with the Italian flair he so beautifully used to express himself, though he never admitted to that. As letters were exchanged, we grew closer, gaining knowledge of each other's lives. Sometimes, when I asked about their parent's lives, Saveria would respond that their lives were very personal and it would be left at that. While I understood, I was disappointed because I still had the urge to know all there was to know about the captain as a person, not just as a name. I will be forever in debt to the mayor of Trapani for his interest in helping to locate the Adragna family. As fate would have it, Giuseppe had an unlisted telephone number and was not one of the Adragnas to receive the inquiry letter. And, Franco was right - not one of the seventy-three Adragnas we sent letters to ever responded.

Franco Di Gangi, translator, holds letter received from mayor of Trapani, Sicily.

We found the Fortuna baby.

*   *   *   *   *

Trapani, Sicily - March - 1985

A heartfelt thank you goes out to our interpreter, Turiddu. It was only through his willingness to act as our interpreter that we survived in Sicily at all. The words "everyone in Italy speaks English" did not apply to Trapani. Without his constant translation of the stories told by Saveria and Giuseppe, I would not have much of a story to write.

"Attention, please. All passengers aboard TWA Flight #840 prepare for landing." The "Fasten Seat Belt" sign flashed on and its annoying beep echoed through the cabin. "Welcome to DaVinci Airport in Rome." Italy. To me, the thought of being thousands of miles from home suddenly seemed like a crazy idea; if I were back in New Jersey, at least I could speak the language. I was thankful that Greg had decided to come along to add moral support as I moved forward into the next phase of my *Fortuna* research.

I have always called New Jersey "home," leaving only briefly for family vacations, but never for a foreign country. Why wasn't I going to France where at least my limited high school French studies might have prepared me for the trip? I did take a short course in Italian at the local adult education school, hoping it would help, but finished the class feeling less than confident in my ability to carry on an intelligent conversation. I never was very good at foreign languages and soon learned that hadn't changed. I could read the words better than I could speak them, but aside from a menu or two, that wouldn't help me very much. Not on this trip. So, why was I sitting on a plane ready to land in Italy? I must have asked myself that question at least a dozen times. And the answer was always the same: I was going to meet the *Fortuna* baby.

As I glanced out the window, I caught a glimpse of Rome and the ancient ruins that dotted the countryside below. Towards the north I spotted the large white ruin which afforded Greg, who was seated in the aisle seat next to me, the opportunity to expound upon the history of not just the Coliseum, but the entire Roman Empire. I was not particularly interested in hearing about the emperors of Rome and their troubled lives, but I welcomed the distraction. Then my mind began to wander to a person of Italian descent whose life I found far more interesting. I was about to land in Italy to meet the *Fortuna* baby, now a grown woman seventy-five years old, who, much like me, still lived in the area where she grew up and had always returned to after her brief vacations. Can you imagine a full-grown woman, seventy-five years old still being called "the baby"? She probably could not, but to the people back in New Jersey who only know of her through the recorded history of the *Fortuna*, she will always be referred to as "the baby."

From Rome we boarded a commuter plane for a short flight to the little airport in Trapani. With only a bump or two, it was considered a smooth landing in the eyes of seasoned fliers. When the "Fasten Seat Belt" signs went off, we were free to gather our belongings and deplane. Within seconds, the aisles were jammed with passengers reaching for luggage that had been tightly packed into the overhead compartments. Everyone was in a hurry, pushing and rushing to meet their friends and loved ones already waiting for them at the gate. And me? I was purposely lagging behind, not exactly sure that I wanted to get off the plane at all. I took a deep breath, summoned my courage and followed the mass of humanity as it flowed along the corridor to a crowded lobby.

"Saveria!" I called out, immediately spotting her in the crowd of well wishers. It was easy to recognize her. She still looked the same as in the picture when she was seven years old. I rushed towards her, with arms outstretched like the plane on which we had just landed. "Signora Carole," she echoed in return, reaching up to embrace me. To make it easier for her to recognize me among the passengers, I had described what I would be wearing, and also told her to look for my husband Greg, who at a bit over six-feet, four-inches tall, would be easy to spot above the crowd. There was not a moment lost in picking each other out of the crowd.

Saveria was somewhat smaller than I'd expected, barely measuring five feet tall, and every inch of her, a lady. She had dressed with great care that morning, knowing how important first impressions are. Her blue silk dress, though simple in style, added a sense of elegance to her small rounded body. Around her shoulders was draped a modest fur cape that added presence to her delicate frame and richness to her appearance. She wore large, clear framed glasses that overpowered the delicate features of her face, reflecting the tenderness of her smile. In her face I could see the same gentle look of her father, mostly around the eyes. Although she looked every one of her seventy five years, to me she was still "the baby."

"Bella, Bella," she joyfully greeted me, gazing up into my face. Instantly we "connected" and at that moment it no longer seemed like a crazy idea to go to Italy. I was now more excited than ever to talk with Saveria and really get to know her. I could tell by the expression in her eyes and warmth that she generated that this was the beginning of a deep and loving friendship.

The next few moments were a blur. I tried to catch a familiar Italian phrase or two, but in all the excitement of our first meeting, my mind drew a blank. Suddenly, I felt my arm being tugged by someone who seemed eager for my attention. When I turned around, I recognized my assailant.

"Giuseppe!" I shouted as we quickly exchanged a kiss on each cheek. He was tall, like his father, standing over six feet, and I would guess that he weighed somewhere around two hundred and thirty pounds. Forgetting that we did not speak the same language, he chatted as though we had passed the Berlitz course with flying colors. I was feeling a bit sorry for Greg. At least I had studied a little Italian and managed to catch a familiar word or two here and there; Greg was lost at "buon giorno."

To my surprise, I heard my name being called above the voices in the crowd. "Carole Bradshaw? Carole, over here." I wondered if it were part of a dream that someone here in Italy knew me and really was speaking English. He was indeed real, and he gestured for me to come towards him.

"I am Turiddu. I am a friend of Signor Giuseppe and I will be available to help while you are visiting here in Trapani for whatever times you might need me." These were the welcomed words of our interpreter. Turiddu was a small man, even smaller than Saveria. He was born in Sicily but left after the war to study in the United States. He spent nearly a decade in California which gave him an extensive vocabulary and a feel for American ways. If I were a religious person, I would have offered my own prayer of thanks to the Madonna of Trapani for sending us Turiddu.

Giuseppe guided us to his car, parked rather haphazardly in a nearby vacant lot. From there we could see the entire Trapani Airport: one tiny building sitting on top of a small clearing in the middle of an overgrown grassy field. There were two black-topped runways marked with faded white lines. It was a very small town; the setting, quite rural. We could have been somewhere in Kansas.

The ride to our hotel was a little frightening. Giuseppe was excited to be hosting his American visitors and seemed a bit distracted as he drove. I remember remarking to Greg that I didn't know they drove on the "wrong side of the road" in Italy, and I distinctly recall his telling me, "They don't." I later learned that as a former ambulance driver, Giuseppe had an impeccable driving record and could always be counted on to be the first to arrive at his destination and always without incident. When we arrived at our hotel, Giuseppe and Turiddu appeared to be quite amused. They had recommended that we stay at The Hotel Astoria, but our travel agent could not find a listing for it and booked us at the Casa Bianca instead. We walked about one hundred steps up a rocky cliff to the hotel entrance that hung above the coastline of the Mediterranean. Turiddu assisted as we checked in, explaining to the clerk that we were from America and that neither of us could speak Italian. They laughed as we got into the small, dingy elevator to take us up to the third floor. Our room was sparsely furnished and dimly lit. There was a double bed, two chairs and a wardrobe. The bathroom was well appointed, and the towels were both numerous and plush. Giuseppe examined every corner of the room, obviously annoyed that we had second guessed him in selecting our accommodations. He and Saveria had recommended the Hotel Astoria because they wanted their guests to stay in the best hotel Trapani had to offer. For us, the Casa Bianca was just fine. It was not luxurious, but its location was good, the price was right, and we would only be calling it home for a few days. Turiddu finally asked how it was that we chose to stay at the Casa Bianca. I briefly explained the situation. Giuseppe snickered as they enjoyed their private joke.

The city of Trapani did not appear to be all that prosperous. Due to its location in the northwest corner of Sicily, the port no longer attracted a high volume of large shipping vessels. The island's other seaport in Catania, on the eastern coast, flourished while Trapani continued to fall farther and farther behind the times. There were several fish canneries nearby, their yards cluttered with piles of discarded fishing gear. Many boats up on blocks undergoing repair crowded the boatyard. Along the narrow streets in town, a few workers dressed in heavy woolen coats were going about their daily chores. I felt like I had been transported back in time seventy-five years to 1909 when the *Fortuna* would have been one of the ships docked in this port.

The long hours of travel, lack of sleep and excitement of the day began to take its toll. Yet, we continued with our schedule. We had only three days in Trapani and we wanted to make the most of them. Sleep would have to come later. Our first stop was the Adragna home where Nina, Giuseppe's sister-in-law, greeted us at the doorway and escorted us up the two flights of stairs to their apartment. It was modestly furnished, decorated with cherished family heirlooms. The walls were bare, except for two large photographs that hung side by side over the mantle: one of their father and one of their mother. I was drawn to the large piano that sat off in the corner, covered with family portraits and treasured souvenirs from their years of travel. I asked who plays the piano, and was told that, as a child, Saveria studied the piano, and admitted to having played quite well. Her mother had given her the piano as a gift, and when her mother died, she stopped playing. That was thirty three years ago.

Tragedy was no stranger to the Adragna family. Both of Saveria's sisters died at a very early age; Anna at 14, and Antonina when she was 28. Her mother and father died when Saveria was in her early forties. During her early childhood, she had been instructed by her father to "look after your brother while I am out at sea." That meant teaching him manners and taking care of his needs. Though she was a child herself, she said she enjoyed looking after Giuseppe. This role had created the extreme closeness they share to this day. Saveria worked as a secretary in a local hospital, an organization that offered many traveling plans to its employees. In her younger days she traveled through Europe, and even made a trip to Egypt. At one time, she was scheduled to travel to America, but the organization folded and the trip was cancelled. Saveria believed she inherited her love of travel from her father. And, also like her father, she fell in love only once, when she was in her mid-twenties. When her fiancé became seriously ill, she devoted herself to caring for him until he died eighteen months later. I detected a slight quiver in Saveria's voice as she told me she never again met anyone she loved so much, so she never married. She then devoted herself to her career.

Giuseppe, the only son of Giovan and Maria, showed the strong facial features of his mother. Though he was tall like his father, the similarities ended there. Unlike the other men of his family, he had no interest at all in a life centered on the seaport. The days of big sailing ships had pretty much come to an end when Giuseppe was born. Shortly after graduating from high school, he was called into the army and sent to Abyssinia (present day Ethiopia and Eritrea). Just when he was about to be discharged, World War II broke out so he remained in the army. He was taken prisoner and sent to a concentration camp in Kenya before being transferred to London. Giuseppe was liberated at the end of World War II and finally rejoined the family in Trapani in 1946. He worked as an administrator at a hospital in Trapani for many years before retiring at age sixty.

We exchanged pleasantries over tea and pastries. I could taste the anisette flavoring so often associated with Italian sweets. (It is not one of my favorites.) There were times when Turiddu was not with us and we were on our own to converse with each other. At first the language differences were a problem, but before long we were communicating with hand gestures and my small but labored attempts at Italian. It was easier than expected. Giuseppe motioned for me and Greg to follow him into another room towards the back of the apartment where he introduced us to his wife, Maria, now confined to bed after first suffering a broken hip and more recently a stroke that had left her paralyzed. Maria and Giuseppe, who have no children, share the apartment with Saveria. Maria's sister, Nina, would often come to spend time with her while Saveria and Giuseppe tended to their daily activities.

After a long day touring the city of Trapani, we returned to our hotel, exhausted from hours of travel and lack of sleep. There was no heat turned on in the room and it felt chilly. Temperatures in March were usually quite warm on this part of the coast, but this year, as luck would have it, the season had been colder than usual. Still dressed in our warm winter coats, we laid down on the bed to catch a few winks before dinner. We woke up well rested - six hours later. We had missed dinner, and it was too early for breakfast, so we decided to call it a night and rest up for the next busy day.

Early the next morning, I called Giuseppe on the phone to let him know we were ready to start the day. My limited Italian vocabulary was enough to know that "pronto" meant hello, and "venti minuti" twenty minutes. Twenty minutes later, Giuseppe pulled up in his car with Saveria proudly seated in the back and Turiddu in the passenger's seat up front. On the top of my "to do" list for the day was to visit the cemetery where Giovan Adragna was buried. Speaking through Turiddu, I asked Giuseppe if he knew somewhere along the way where I could buy some flowers to place at the grave site. Giuseppe gave a hearty laugh which soon needed no further explanation. Around the bend, right in front of the gate leading into the cemetery, were at least thirty flower stands lining the avenue like parking meters on a New York City street. We stopped at a particularly colorful stand where Giuseppe and Saveria chose some vibrant red carnations, obviously a favorite of either themselves or their father. Giuseppe explained to the merchant that "this young lady and her man came all the way from America to see where my father is buried." The young man at the stand smiled and presented me with a big bouquet of daisies, my favorite flower, which I later placed on the grave of Giovan Adragna.

We walked through the gate of the cemetery, barely able to keep pace with Saveria. As I walked through the cemetery, I couldn't help but notice that many of the graves had framed photos of the deceased attached to the headstone. I was not sure if this was a European, Italian or Catholic tradition- or perhaps all three. We followed Saveria down a narrow path, rounding several corners before arriving at the tomb of her father. It was a lovely spot, located in an older section undisturbed by the newer, modern-type tombs. His tomb was set on a corner, giving him importance when approached from either direction. I stood next to Saveria and watched as she and Giuseppe gently laid their flowers in place, remembering their father with deep affection. At the moment I stood in front of his tomb reading the names and dates inscribed on the stone, Captain Giovan Adragna became a real person to me for the first time. I could actually feel his presence. At first I was a little startled when I saw the photograph of Giovan Adragna attached to his headstone. It had been taken when he was well into his seventies, maybe even his eighties, and he no longer resembled the man I first saw in the family photo. Though he looked like a stranger, I still felt a connection to this man whom I had known only through pictures and documents. After so many years, his story and my quest for knowledge had brought us together to meet at this place. It was a very moving moment. I let Saveria and Giuseppe walk ahead of me so, out of respect, they would not see me taking pictures of their father's headstone. Clearly inscribed on the stone were the dates of his birth and death (1867-1954); I would take this information back home to prove that Captain Adragna had not committed suicide at age forty three as reported back in 1910, but lived a long and productive life until his death in 1954 at age eighty seven.

After leaving the cemetery, Giuseppe knew exactly where he would take us next. He showed genuine amusement in his selection of the next "tourist attraction" and wasted no time driving there. "Hotel Astoria! Hotel Astoria!" Giuseppe exclaimed as Saveria and Turiddu grinned. "You see, it really does exist," Turiddu pointed out. Oh yes, it did indeed exist. And it was truly a beautiful, large, white, sprawling building nestled on the glistening white sandy beach along the clear blue water of the Mediterranean. It was an elegant setting. No wonder Giuseppe was disappointed with our choice of the Casa Bianca. Now I understood the private joke he shared with Turiddu.

From the Hotel Astoria parking lot, we drove up the coast, taking in the magnificent views along the way. The color of the water was sapphire blue, much like you would see on a travel brochure, and it looked clean enough to drink. Though well into the month of March, spring had not yet arrived. But, this was still the Mediterranean, and I was excited to see it, with or without the spring flowers.

Our next stop was one Saveria and Giuseppe knew I would be most excited to visit: the harbor. It was obvious they knew it well. Giuseppe motioned for me to come close to the edge of the pier where he was standing. Again, speaking through the translated words of Turiddu, Giuseppe told us "This is where our father's ship, the *Fortuna*, was tied up. Just about right here." There was no plaque that said "the *Fortuna* was tied up here," but I knew from his tone that he knew he was right. In the distance I could see a lighthouse, the one which seventy-five years before had cleared the way for the *Fortuna's* final voyage. Standing in that spot sent chills up my spine. For a moment, I closed my eyes and could see the harbor filled with the towering masts of big sailing ships, some undergoing repair, others ready to make their silent journey out into the ocean. I could almost hear the excited voices of the crews as they prepared the ship for their next voyage. And, as I stood on the dock, I thought of the *Fortuna*, about to embark on the long journey to an event that some day in the future, would bring them into my life.

*   *   *   *   *

By now Greg and I were more than just friends to Saveria and Giuseppe. We were a part of their family, including Turiddu. We had dined together and exchanged stories one would only share with family. Back in the comfort of their apartment, we relaxed and again turned our conversation back to the early days of the *Fortuna* and Saveria's recollections and memories of her father as a man, and also as the captain of the ship. I knew we had been accepted into their family when Saveria now answered all those questions she once thought to be too personal.

"My father comes from a long line of sea captains," Saveria explained through the voice of Turiddu. "His father, and also his father's father were sea captains, too. And so were his two brothers, Vito and Antonino. So it did not seem strange that he would follow the sea, too." Giuseppe got up and disappeared into the other room and returned with a large frame under his arm. "Here. This is his diploma," he said as he handed me the old, gesso-framed document. Issued by Umberto University in Trapani in 1884, this diploma was awarded to Giovan Battista Adragna certifying him as 'capitano di lungo corso', meaning that he could sail the waters of both hemispheres. Saveria explained "there were two different kinds of degrees to study for. One gave you the right to sail only as far as the Straits of Gibraltar, the other was unlimited. It gave permission to sail all the waters of the globe. This was the one my father possessed. He could sail all over the world. I am not sure when he made the trips, but I do remember his telling me that he had sailed around the world three times. He was a marvelous captain, highly respected by all his fellow seamen, and by people who employed him." It was obvious that Saveria, too, was very proud of his ability to master the big ships of those times.

"My father had been away for a long time, about two years," Saveria continued. "He came home for only about a month then sailed again to Marseille, France. By this time, my mother wanted no more of the lonely life she had for the past two years. She missed him a lot. They were so much in love, just like newlyweds all the time. It was difficult for them to be separated. After he left for Marseille, my mother decided that she did not want to spend another two years alone, so she and my sisters, Anna and Antonina, went to Marseille to meet him. After the wreck of the *Fortuna*, my father continued to sail for different companies for many years, but he never sailed outside of the Straits. In 1939, when he was seventy two years old, he made his last sailing trip from Trapani to Naples on a job that other captains had refused because it was considered too difficult. The wreck of the *Fortuna* was a sad day in my father's life and career, and as we were growing up, we never, ever spoke of it in our family. It was only in his older years when he would reminisce about the past that my father shared stories about the disaster with family and friends. I do know that he was still considered a good captain. And he was a very good husband and father."

Carole meets Saveria, the Fortuna baby,
in her home in Trapani.

Carole feels Captain
Adragna's presence
as she stands next to
his photograph.

Pictured is his diploma
from Umberto University
where he received his
degree to sail all waters
of the world.

Tomb of
Giovan Adragna
in
Trapani, Sicily

Note the date:

He did not commit suicide
as was reported in 1910.

He died in Trapani in
1954 at age 87.

*   *   *   *   *

Long Beach Island - 1985

The main reason I traveled to Trapani was to meet the *"Fortuna baby"* and see if she was interested in traveling to Ship Bottom for the dedication of the *Fortuna's* anchor. After meeting her in person, there was no question that she was physically able. But was she interested in coming to Ship Bottom? When I asked Saveria that, if we were able to raise the money to buy the plane ticket for her to come to America, would she like to come? She did not have to think long before answering.

"There are only two places where I would really like to visit. One is to see Barbados where I was born. The other is to return to the town where I was carried from my father's wrecked ship," Saveria told us as she struggled to hold back her tears. That was all I needed to know. Somehow, we would raise the money to fly Saveria and Giuseppe to America so they could attend the dedication of their father's anchor.

It was time to be creative. By this time, I was perfectly comfortable with asking for help and turned to those who could be the most helpful in supplying airplane tickets. My letter to Alitalia Airlines, dated April 25, 1985, began with the words of Saveria, the star of this story: *"I would really like to return to the place in America where I was rescued from the wrecked ship of my father when I was a month and two weeks old, and to be present when the monument is dedicated in his honor"*, and went on to tell the whole story of the *Fortuna*. On May 21, 1985, Alitalia Airlines confirmed that they would provide a free ticket for the *"Fortuna* baby" to fly to J.F.K. Airport in New York. The Ship Bottom Civic Association graciously offered to pay for Giuseppe's plane ticket.

During the summer, plans were formalized for the combined ceremony to celebrate Ship Bottom's 60th Anniversary and the dedication of the *Fortuna's* anchor. The mayors of many surrounding towns, New Jersey State senators and representatives, and officials of local civic organizations were invited to attend. On August 15, 1985 I sent a letter to President Ronald Reagan inviting him to attend the ceremony. On September 4, he sent a response. Though he appreciated the opportunity to attend, he expressed his regret that because of heavy demands on his schedule, he would be unable to attend. Confident that we had extended invitations to all the right people, we focused our attention on constructing the monument.

It was necessary to put off building the monument until after the summer tourist season was over. That left only three weeks to construct the monument and put the anchor in its place. Paul Buterick, still feeling a strong connection to the anchor, donated the pilings needed as footings to support the great weight of the anchor, and the labor and use of the equipment to drive them in. It was the same equipment he used to wrest the anchor from its sandy grave. Few of the workers who volunteered were under age sixty-five, but as such, they had lifetimes of experience to bring to the project. John Guld, who has served the borough zoning board for over twenty years, had spent forty years in the concrete masonry business. He prepared the plywood forms into which the concrete would be poured. Marvin Cranmer, born and raised in the area, applied his skill as a carpenter. And, no one should have been surprised at the force with which Mayor Bob Nissen could swing a sledge hammer to pound in stakes. Tom Feeney, a local contractor, donated a few yards of excess cement from one of his trucks which cut down considerably on the expense. Immediately following the final troweling of the pad, those involved became concerned that the wet cement might be desecrated. Stanley "Bart" Smullen applied the administrative skills developed over many years of public service in Philadelphia to stand guard so that no one could write their initials in the wet cement before it hardened. But, moments after he left, in the darkness of the night, a person who *thinks* he remains anonymous came and set one of the *Fortuna's* salvaged skylights into the wet cement. Tuckerton Lumber Co., in Surf City, donated the wood for the posts, and Greg hand-shaped the tops of each one before securing them to the cement pad. He then drilled holes and fastened the plaques to finish the posts. The final touch to the monument - a colorful mosaic-tile rendering of the *Fortuna* standing upright on the beach - would be added later by an Italian tile worker who "just had to be a part of the historic event." When completed, the monument was absolutely beautiful.

*   *   *   *   *

September 23, 1985

Alitalia Airlines Flight Number 642 from Rome arrived at J.F. Kennedy Airport in New York right on schedule. As the passengers disembarked, the fourth person off the plane and through the gate was Giuseppe, as big as life and ready to greet the world. Saveria tentatively followed behind, as though she was not too sure she wanted to be here at all. It would be the first time in his life that Giuseppe had visited the United States. For Saveria, it would be the second. She was excited to be living one of her lifetime dreams of returning to the place where she was carried off her father's shipwreck when she was just an infant.

Romano D'Angelo, the representative from Alitalia Airlines on hand to officially greet Saveria and Giuseppe, spotted them in line and personally escorted them to the baggage claim area where their luggage had already cleared customs. Italian words were flowing in every direction and, try as I might, I didn't understand a single word! Classroom Italian and conversational Italian in real-time, with its own dialect, are like two different languages. Saveria and Giuseppe were very excited to be in America and wondered if everyone who came to visit America was greeted with such importance.

The airport welcome was more relaxed than our first meeting in Trapani. This was more like a reunion, but I was still anxious. We were the hosts this time, responsible for their well-being while they were visiting the States. My six week Italian mini-course helped a little with the pronunciation of the 1000 nouns I remembered, but I couldn't keep up with their fast paced conversations. Before long, we all realized that hand signals and gestures were all we needed, and we managed to get along just fine.

We greeted each other with the hugs of long lost relatives, relieved that the trip had gone so smoothly. My seven year old son, Jonathan, presented Saveria with the bouquet of flowers he'd picked out himself, just for her: red and white carnations with plenty of greens, representing the colors of the Italian flag. In the middle of the bouquet were a small American flag and his homemade sign that read "Benveniti Saveria e Giuseppe," which to them said "welcome." Saveria was very touched and kissed Jonathan on the cheek. Within minutes we were joined by Julie, Joe and Joe Previto Jr., Saveria and Giuseppe's relatives who live in New York. Joe presented their plan. Saveria and Giuseppe would be spending three days with the Previtos in New York; that would give them a few days to adjust to the time change before being thrust into the vigorous schedule we had planned for the upcoming week. Yes, it was a good plan. Everyone in the Previto household spoke Italian, and they were sure to feel comfortable at their home. We said our quick goodbyes almost as quickly as we said our hellos, settled them into the Previto's car and waved goodbye. We would see them again in three days.

Saveria and Giuseppe loved New York. First they saw the Statue of Liberty, but were disappointed that it was partially obscured by the scaffolding around it. At the time, minor restoration was being made in preparation for its 100th anniversary celebration scheduled for 1986. Though disappointed, they were proud to have seen the Statue in person. They visited the Empire State Building where Joseph Previto's law firm has its office, and like real troopers, ventured up to the top. They were equally impressed by the view from the top and the prestigious address of Previto's office.

They saw the city by daylight and again when illuminated at night. The city lights fascinated them; so different from anything they have in Trapani. They wished they could have stayed longer and just watched. As you would expect, the time passed by too quickly as they reminisced about the past, about the life they once shared back home years ago. Joseph Previto's mother was the connection to Saveria and Giuseppe. She once lived in Trapani and was related to their mother, Maria Savona. Mrs. Previto often took care of Giuseppe, looking after him as if he were her own child. She gave him the nickname, Pino.

Saveria and Giuseppe found saying goodbye to the Previtos bittersweet. The time was much too short to catch up on all the years they had been apart, but they would be seeing them again at the dedication festivities. So, it was time to move on. Giuseppe and Saveria were anxious to meet Franco, our beloved translator. Though Franco was translating my English words to them into Italian, I know he inserted his own flavor into the written conversations.

Franco and his wife, Christine, were at his barber shop on Bloomfield Avenue in the heart of Caldwell when we arrived. He knew Saveria and Giuseppe only through photos and letters, but today he felt like he was welcoming "family." Traffic into his shop had ceased during our entire stay as if there were a sign hanging on the door that read "do not enter - I have guests." There was one invited person who did enter the shop: Gene Collerd, the staff photographer from the local newspaper, *The Progress*. He came to photograph the people from Italy who were part of a feature story his newspaper had covered the previous week. As he began to position the people for his photo, he became quite confused. Of course Gene knew who Franco and Christine were. And he knew the baby was a female so, much to Giuseppe's disappointment, Gene did not focus any attention on him at all. It was a toss-up between Saveria and me as to who "the baby" was. I was the youngest one in the shop and Saveria the oldest, topping Gene's age by a decade or so. His guess seemed well founded. "And, you are the baby?" he questioned pointing towards me.

"No, no, no. Not me. She is the baby," I responded guiding him closer to seventy five year old Saveria. We all laughed, Gene shrugged, and then took several pictures for the upcoming issue of the newspaper.

We had lunch at Franco's, (no relation to Franco Di Gangi) a local Italian restaurant, where everyone was comfortable speaking his own language. Our waiter, Pietro, was delighted to converse with our visitors in his native tongue. We told him a shortened version of the *Fortuna* story, and he was both fascinated and disappointed that he wasn't a part of such a great story. I promised Pietro I'd mention him in the book.

I picked Jonathan up at school and headed to the Garden State Parkway for the two hour drive to Long Beach Island. By this time, Saveria was quite exhausted and managed to catch a few winks while resting comfortably in the front seat of the car. Giuseppe was way too curious about his surroundings to sleep. Like an impatient child, he kept asking questions, in Italian: "what are we passing, how much longer, what is a causeway, and why are you throwing your money out the window into those bins?" Without the presence of an interpreter, I answered the questions as best I could with my limited Italian vocabulary, but I hadn't studied how to say I was "throwing money out the window to pay a parkway toll." I'm not sure he fully understood "automatic toll collection."

It was exactly two hours later when we reached the bridge to Long Beach Island. The nice weather we left behind in Caldwell had already turned sour. The sky was gray and a mist was beginning to settle along the shore. The weather forecast was not good. As a matter of fact, it could not have been worse. As the day progressed, radio broadcasters began alerting residents of low lying shore areas to prepare for possible evacuation due to the course of upcoming Hurricane Gloria. It didn't seem much like a hurricane was coming at all. This kind of misty, breezy day was quite typical here on Long Beach Island. We drove across the bridge over Manahawkin Bay, arriving at the boat dock in Ship Bottom at 3:45 p.m. We were greeted by Mayor Nissen and a small crowd of townspeople who had gathered at the dock. A huge red, white and green banner resembling the Italian flag stretched between two poles, sporting the words "Benvenuti Saveria e Giuseppe a Ship Bottom," welcomed them. They were touched by the celebration of their arrival but had not yet understood their treatment as celebrities.

The moment was very exciting for Saveria and Giuseppe, for me, and for the people of Ship Bottom. It isn't every day that a woman who was part of an historic disaster returns to the scene to talk about it. This was to be a time of celebration, yet we could not overlook the activity in the background. There were boats lined up fifteen to twenty at a time, waiting to be lifted out of the water and put on trailers to be transported away from the coast to safer harbors. The hurricane warning was out and people were taking the necessary precautions. We would have to keep a close watch on the weather.

The house where Saveria and Giuseppe were to stay during their visit was graciously offered by Pat Jeffrey, the borough clerk and resident of Ship Bottom. Flowers in red, white and blue decorated the coffee table, and the kitchen had been well stocked with edibles for our guests, should they get hungry during the night. They were pleased with their accommodations and surprised that someone would turn their own home over to strangers. This was just the first of many times they would be shown they were indeed not strangers but family in the hearts of the people of Ship Bottom.

On their first night in Ship Bottom, Saveria and Giuseppe were the honored guests of Ship Bottom's Mayor, Bob Nissen and his wife, Pat. The Nissens live in a lovely home on the bayside in Ship Bottom with their dog, Max and rabbit, Pansy. Their only son, Jan, had moved into his own quarters nearby and returned to join the group for dinner. Dinner guests for the evening included me, Jonathan and Greg, who due to unplanned meetings at work could not reach the beach in time to attend; Ed and Zena Toriello, members of the Italian American Club of Stafford; and Mario Cesare, the Long Beach Island barber who assisted with translations while I was on the Island during the summer months, and who would again translate the evening's conversations for us. The dinner table was beautifully set with Pat's finest antique china and silver; its elegance allowed one to imagine we would be dining with the President of the United States! The aroma of Italian seasonings coming from the kitchen offered promise of a tasty homemade meal which was subsequently delivered. That was just the way Pat did things. She was always the perfect hostess. Pat did not speak any Italian whatsoever, so she just spoke to Saveria and Giuseppe in English and waited to be translated by either Ed or Mario. Everything was going along very smoothly, and our guests were thoroughly enjoying their first day in Ship Bottom. But Bob, usually very attentive to his guests, was easily distracted by the voices on his CB scanner, the one that kept him in constant contact with the police departments on the Island. As a town official, it was imperative that he be kept updated on the rapidly approaching hurricane. By early Thursday evening, Hurricane Gloria had intensified to a Category 4 near the Bahamas, and Long Beach Island was in its direct path. Not only was it to hit the Island, but it was to hit with such force that there was the strong possibility the Island would not be there after she passed through.

Halfway through dinner, the tone of our conversations changed from light-hearted to serious as the violent storm rapidly headed our way. It was expected that within the next few hours, New Jersey's governor, Thomas Kean, would issue a mandatory evacuation order to all Island residents. We discussed the situation among ourselves in English so we would not alarm our guests. We began making plans for an impending evacuation. Ed and Zena Toriello who lived in Manahawkin, a more or less safer place to be in the event of a hurricane, offered to have Saveria and Giuseppe spend the night with them. They had plenty of room, and they also could speak Italian and ease any fears they might have. It would be best to get them off the Island right away, before the storm, rather than make a hasty escape in the middle of the night. By then the bay waters would probably already have flooded the streets, making it impossible to get off the Island. Everyone noticed that

Saveria appeared to be very distressed. She kept saying, in Italian, the same words over and over quietly to herself. Most of us did not know what she was saying, but Ed did. He quickly translated her words for us: "The last time I came to Ship Bottom was during a violent storm that caused my father's ship to be lost. This time I come back again to another violent storm." She shook her head and repeated the words over and over again.

The mandatory evacuation order came at around 11:00 p.m. This meant the storm was due to hit us head on and we'd better make plans not to be here when it does. Saveria and Giuseppe had already left to spend the night with the Toriellos in Manahawkin and it was time for the rest of us to secure our homes and prepare to evacuate. Anything and everything that could become flying objects either needed to be tied down or brought inside. Jonathan and I dragged the gas grill, patio furniture and trash cans into the house, and tied the sailboat and trailer securely between two trees. We were expecting and preparing for the worst. By the time Greg arrived a short time later, most of the people had already left the Island. We've all learned from previous experience that before the actual force of the hurricane arrives, the water in the bay backs up and floods the boulevard, the only road off the Island. I called my friend, Dale Gray, who lives on the mainland in Tuckerton, and she graciously invited us to weather the storm at her home. Jonathan was terrified at the thought of being trapped on Long Beach Island in the middle of a dangerous hurricane and was already sitting in the car waiting for us to leave. Greg, who secretly longed to "wait out the storm," carefully listened to the weather report and decided this one was for real and he, too, was ready to leave.

Our accommodations at Dale's were camp-style. The large living room was lined with folding cots and sleeping bags being used by others who had fled their homes for safer quarters. Early Friday morning, the phone lines went dead, but the television coverage continued. We watched the storm waves break over the boardwalk thirty miles away in Atlantic City, and to breach the inland waterways in areas along the coast south of Long Beach Island. As the storm came closer, it looked like it had its sights on Long Beach Island, too. But, at the last minute, Hurricane Gloria took a sudden turn to the east and the worst of her went out to sea. The entire Island was flooded, and many, many feet of sand had washed away from the beach, but because the hurricane came at the time of low tide, the Island had been spared total devastation. Immediately after the hurricane passed over, the sun came out, though the strong winds continued for several hours. By early afternoon, the road blocks were lifted and residents could return to the Island to check their houses and return home. I sat in the line of cars on the causeway waiting to get back onto the Island for several hours. When I finally reached the end of the causeway in Ship Bottom, I wondered how I would even get home. The roads were still flooded, too deep for my small Toyota Celica to drive through. I found the highest spot in the road and drove through two feet of water, hoping the engine wouldn't conk out half way through. It didn't. I made it through to a dry street and drove home, relieved to see that our house had weathered the storm. The ocean had crested the dune and met the water from the bay half-way up our street, bringing all sorts of debris along with it. Anything that would float, did. We had seaweed from the bay in our front yard. Large telephone poles had floated from who knows where. Boats had been blown out of the bay into the street, against buildings, or just blown through the air until they landed, splintering into hundreds of pieces. Hurricane Gloria, dubbed the "Storm of the Century" by Neil Frank of the National Hurricane Center, had shown her presence, but she didn't take the Island with her.

While staying with Zena and Ed, Saveria and Giuseppe had witnessed, firsthand, the force of a hurricane, an all too real-life example of a storm like the one that claimed the *Fortuna* many years before. As the storm passed over Ed and Zena's house, a strong gust of wind ripped one of the windows in their room right off its metal hinges and bent it like it was a piece of aluminum foil. To Giuseppe and Saveria, Ed and Zena were the present day lifesavers who saved them from disaster that night when they carried them off the Island before the terrific storm.

*   *   *   *   *

Ed and Zena were a little late arriving at the Italian American Club facilities with Saveria and Giuseppe, the honored guests for a testimonial dinner. In spite of the harrowing time they'd spent with Hurricane Gloria the previous night, they looked well rested. Saveria looked quite elegant in her black and white print dress, adorned by a beautiful corsage, compliments of Bob Cooper of the Cedar Garden. Both Saveria and Giuseppe felt so relaxed among so many people speaking their language; it was like being part of one big family. The evening was filled with introductions, delicious food, dancing, touching speeches, and many of tears of joy.

Reading slowly from her hand written words on the folded piece of paper, Saveria softly spoke the words she held within her heart:

(English Translation)

Mr. Mayor, Officials and Friends,

I am taken by such deep emotions that it is difficult for me to speak, and I ask for you to forgive me. My brother and I want to express our deep appreciation to the authorities and to the people of this grand and hospitable land for your manifestation of affection, and we want to thank you for joining us in this great celebration. A very special thank you to the various heads of the committees and the members of the Stafford Italian American Club who by sponsoring this elegant dinner, have clearly demonstrated a deep sense of friendliness and patriotism. We also wish to thank Mr. and Mrs. Toriello for their kind dinner invitation.

We are very happy to have had the opportunity to meet such marvelous people who have bestowed upon us all their kindness and love, making us feel like citizens of this wonderful land of yours, and making us forget, briefly, our beloved Trapani.

Allow me to extend a very deep feeling of love and gratitude to a very affectionate, generous and untiring person who because of all her hard work and interest in this project has made it possible for us to be present tonight, and receive all these loving manifestations. Carole, for the rest of our lives, you will remain always in our hearts. It is because of your endeavors that the memory of our father will live forever in this land. We are certain that even at this moment he is blessing you. Carole, it is because of you that after seventy five years I am in the land where I was rescued. Destiny and fate are in the hands of God, but sometimes God selects one special person to make his plans materialize. Who could have imagined that you would come to Trapani to meet us personally?

You should be proud of all your endeavors because as you can see - we are here!

We will cherish forever these hours spent together. We cannot find words to express our deepest gratitude and appreciation to all of you present here, and we assure you that the memory of this moment will be forever in our hearts.

I want to thank personally my dear Franco Di Gangi for all his collaboration and we will remember him dearly.

My brother and I send all of you a warm and affectionate embrace, and a kiss that I am going to give to Carole is meant for all of you.

Saveria and Giuseppe Adragna

After listening to Saveria's speech, there was no doubt in anyone's mind that by coming back to Ship Bottom to be a part of the celebration, their lives would be changed forever.

As touched as we all were by the kind words of joy and appreciation expressed by Saveria, there was still something missing. No one had heard from Giuseppe. He was coaxed and prodded several times to make a speech, but each time he refused. Someone, and I honestly don't remember who, decided to take matters into his own hands and literally put a microphone in front of Giuseppe, motioning for him to say a few words. Not knowing exactly what to say or how to say it, he rose from his chair and, without the use of a microphone, bellowed the words "thank you very much" in perfect English. The crowd went wild! That was the first and last time we heard Giuseppe speak English, and it was worth every minute of the wait.

By this time I had come to expect the unexpected, but I was unprepared for the next surprise. Marvin Cranmer, a long time resident of Ship Bottom, stepped up to the podium where Saveria was still standing and without the slightest display of showmanship, simply handed her a neatly wrapped nine inch square package. With all eyes watching as she nervously removed the paper wrapper, a sudden gasp came from the crowd as she held up her gift. It was a whole tile that had been carried aboard the *Fortuna* as ballast at the time it became a wreck on the beach in Ship Bottom in 1910. The tile, now more than seventy five years old, still showed the inscription "Arnaud Etienne & Cie St. Henry Marseille" as clearly as if it had just been engraved yesterday. The red tile, like the piece that had started the re-birth of the *Fortuna* several years before, had come around full circle. We all took a moment to dry our eyes and collect our composure.

This anchor is "Dedicated in honor of those who sailed and lost their lives in these treacherous waters of Long Beach Island and to the crews of the lifesaving stations who risked their own lives in heroic efforts to save others."

Saturday, September 28, 1985

The plans for the dedication ceremony were scheduled to go on as arranged, with the exception of the parade. Advance notice had to be given to the participants, so it was cancelled when the hurricane was predicted to hit Long Beach Island. The fireworks scheduled for the evening were postponed until the following weekend. Everything else was a "go."

Saturday morning, two days after the storm passed through, was a beautiful day. The sky was the color blue you would have chosen if you could pick a shade yourself. There were clouds so white they looked more than three dimensional against the clear blue sky. It was a perfect day to celebrate Ship Bottom's 60th Anniversary, the Dedication of the *Fortuna* Anchor, and Hurricane Gloria's departure. Yes, it was a day to celebrate.

In our haste to evacuate Saveria and Giuseppe from Ship Bottom, we suddenly realized that they still had not seen the anchor from their father's ship. But, they must wait. Earlier in the morning I had covered the anchor with a big white cloth that would remain until later in the ceremony when Saveria and Giuseppe would clip the ties that held it in place, exposing the monument to them for the first time.

Our pre-ceremony interviews were scheduled to begin at nine o'clock. These segments would be used for the lead into the taped coverage of the ceremony that would later be televised on the local TV station by TKR cable. The introduction to the ceremony and interviews of key players would be conducted by Long Beach Island historian, John Bailey Lloyd. Mayor Nissen was the first to be interviewed. Of course, there were questions about the upcoming anniversary celebration and the dedication ceremony, but he also commented on the aftermath of Hurricane Gloria. After assuring the audience that the town had survived the hurricane, Mayor Nissen turned the microphone over to me, The Anchor Lady. Most of what I wanted to say was in my prepared speech for the main part of the program, but I had to say something for my interview. I don't remember exactly what I said; something to the effect that these storms have a silver lining, and if it weren't for the courageous actions of the lifesavers in saving those on board the *Fortuna*, the children of the ship's captain would not be here today to dedicate this anchor.

Just as I had finished my interview, I was pulled aside by the Ship Bottom Postmaster. He pointed to the black limousine parked in the driveway, and told me there was someone inside who was looking for me. As I approached the vehicle, two men dressed in identical black suits, crisp white shirts and tastefully colored ties got out of the car and walked towards me. They looked very serious, a stark contrast to the happy faces of everyone else in the crowd. When I confirmed that I was Carole Bradshaw, one man handed me a large, manila envelope, said a few words which I can't recall, then got back in the car and slowly drove away. It was only a few minutes later that I noticed the return address in the upper left corner of the envelope: The White House, Washington.

Saveria was growing more and more anxious as the time for her interview drew closer. Franco Di Gangi was the on-the-spot interpreter and, most likely due to all his years' experience in the local Playcrafters Club, a Caldwell group of stage performers, he was not the least bit nervous. Saveria was hesitant about talking into a microphone and nervously answered the questions with short, one or two-word responses. When Franco translated the words everyone had waited seventy five years to hear, he embroidered upon them with the greatest amount of diplomacy. Hearing Saveria speak her own words pleased the crowd to no end. Now that all the "celebrity" interviews had been completed and the guest speakers had assembled on the grandstand, the dedication ceremony was ready to begin.

Saveria and Giuseppe, not quite grasping their own importance in this ceremony, remarked several times to Franco that they were happy to be a part of the program to honor their father. It was their duty as his only living children to accept this honor for him. Although they felt ill at ease being the center of attention, they continued to perform their duty to their loving father.

The ceremony began with an inspiring invocation by Dr. Reverend Neal Raver, a long-time resident of Ship Bottom, who did not forget to thank God for sparing our island from destruction by Hurricane

Gloria. The crowd joined him in thanks. The ceremony was divided into two parts, one giving recognition to the town of Ship Bottom on its 60th anniversary; the other honoring the Adragnas and dedicating the *Fortuna's* anchor. Though separate parts of the ceremony, they were historically intertwined. The wreck of the *Fortuna* was just one of many events in its past that shaped the town of Ship Bottom into that we know today.

Certificates, flags, proclamations and awards were given by various speakers to the town of Ship Bottom in honor of their 60th anniversary. Many meaningful speeches and touching gifts were also given to Saveria and Giuseppe, including the keys to the town of Ship Bottom. A New Jersey state flag was presented on behalf of New Jersey Governor Thomas Kean by his Director of Community Affairs, John P. Renna. Bart Smullen, President of the Ship Bottom Civic Association, presented them with the United States flag and the flag of Long Beach Island. Ed Toriello presented the Italian flag on behalf of the Italian American Club. All these flags were presented specifically to Saveria whose birth seventy five years before was so important to her father that he raised all the flags on his ship to announce her birth. And, now, here in Ship Bottom, we thought she was important enough for us to raise all the flags, too.

The usual speeches followed, filled with praise for the townspeople who worked so hard to provide the labor and resources needed to see the anchor project become a reality. And, there were many kind words of appreciation for The Anchor Lady who started the project two years before. Saveria, in particular, was awestruck by all the special attention they were receiving. After all, it was their father they were here to honor, yet she wondered why they were being treated like celebrities. At the moment Saveria realized that she was a celebrity, she became more relaxed and began to enjoy the attentions of the crowd.

It was now time for Saveria, the *Fortuna* baby, to speak to the crowd. She walked towards the podium, strongly clinging to Franco's arm for both physical and emotional support, then gingerly unfolded several letter-sized pieces of paper upon which she had written her speech. The crowd fell silent as she began to tell how touched she was that all this celebration was taking place, and how much it would have touched her father to see what was being done for him. Franco translated her words and, this time, did not embellish upon any of her speech.

> Good Morning to Everyone,
>
> Our father was a good captain, a good father, and a marvelously courageous man. We are very anxious to see this monument to our father, the man who we loved so much both when he was alive and after his death. We are at the same time proud of him and because of this initiative, he has left an imprint of himself for the future, and this touches our hearts. We thank you all for welcoming us to your town with such festivities, and we thank you for our visit here. On behalf of our father, we thank you for this wonderful celebration, a keepsake of our visit here.
>
> Saveria Fortunata Marina Adragna

Her speech was filled with the deep emotion that only Saveria could express. Midway through her speech, emotions overcame her. Saveria's eyes filled with tears and her voice began to tremble, but she continued and made it through to the end. Her words were gentle. She spoke from her heart.

Hearing "the *Fortuna* baby" speak was a big moment of the celebration, leading up to the unveiling of the anchor. Saveria and Giuseppe, assisted by several Ship Bottom firemen, had the honor of removing the cover to unveil the now famous *Fortuna* anchor. Brian Fullerton, a student at the Long Beach Island grade school, played *Taps* while they fidgeted with the ribbons that fought against being untied. Finally, the cheers went up from the crowd as the curtain was removed revealing the efforts of two years' labor by a lot of dedicated people. It was a spectacular sight, the anchor sitting tall on its pedestal with its arm raised to the sky like that of the Statue of Liberty, as the flags of both the United States and Italy flew intertwined in the breeze above. The moment was captured in our minds and recorded on tape, preserved forever. Saveria and Giuseppe were overcome with emotion as they viewed their father's anchor for the first time. I could not even imagine what they were thinking or feeling. Surely there was joy, but no doubt there was pain as they recalled the circumstances that brought them to Ship Bottom to view it.

And now, it was my turn. My time to let go of the anchor which had occupied so much of my time and energies over the preceding two years. But before I began my speech, there was something I needed to share with the crowd.

"Before I begin my speech, I'd like to read a letter that I just received fifteen minutes before our ceremony started. It is dated September 23, 1985" then I continued to read the letter.

> I am very pleased to send greetings to everyone taking part in the dedication of the anchor from the square-rigger <u>FORTUNA</u>. My particular welcome goes to Signorina Saveria Fortunata Marina Adragna, the only surviving passenger of the wreck of the <u>FORTUNA</u>, and her brother Giuseppe.
>
> The anchor will serve as a reminder of a dramatic event in your community's history. You can take special pride in the fact that so many citizens banded together and raised the funds themselves to mount the anchor in a suitable setting. Your actions demonstrate the kind of community spirit that has done so much to make this country a wonderful place to live.
>
> Nancy joins me in sending best wishes to all for a memorable day. God bless you.
>
> Ronald Reagan

The loud cheers from the crowd confirmed what I already knew: that they were impressed by the words of our President who took the time to honor their town of Ship Bottom.

Realizing how difficult an act that would be to follow, I took my place at the podium, took a deep breath, and greeted the crowd:

> Good Morning, honored guests. Buon giorno, Saveria e Giuseppe. And, welcome to all who are gathered here today to be a part of this historic event.

Before I begin my dedication speech, I would like to say a few words of thanks, especially to my family who has stood by me during this period of near total involvement with this anchor project, and also to the Civic Association who undertook the challenge of fundraising for the construction and completion of this anchor monument.

To get us in the proper mood for this day, I'd like to share with you a story told to me by Saveria. It takes us back seventy-five years to when Captain Adragna, Saveria's father, anchored the *Fortuna* in the Harbor of Barbados to await the birth of his newest child. The captain already had two girls, and everyone was hoping this time the new baby would be a boy. The Harbormaster instructed the captain to raise all the flags on his ship when his new son was born, and the townspeople would come to welcome him. On November 25, 1909 a midwife was summoned aboard the *Fortuna* and a baby girl was delivered to the captain's wife. Captain Adragna ordered all flags on the ship to be raised, and all the townspeople came down to welcome the new son. But when they saw it was just a girl, they were confused. Why raise the flags for another girl? Captain Adragna explained: "I have two other daughters I never saw born, and when I saw this one born, I figured she was worth raising all the flags for." So today, with Saveria back on American soil for only the second time in her entire life, isn't it worth raising the flags for her once again?

Today I feel a bit like Miss America must have felt when she was about to relinquish her crown to the next title holder. During the past year, my attachment to this anchor has been a close one, yet one which has allowed me to travel beyond its location here in Ship Bottom to, literally, the far corners of the globe. Seventy-five years ago when Captain Adragna set sail from his hometown of Trapani, Sicily, little did he know that the voyage would be filled with both joy and sorrow. It was indeed a joyous occasion when en route to New York his wife gave birth to their newest daughter. By her names Fortunata Marina we can tell how deeply he loved his life as a sea captain. But, when the *Fortuna* became a fatal statistic here on our shores of Ship Bottom, New Jersey, his world was shattered. He returned to Trapani with his family and crew, never to learn that his story did not end right there. Many of us have seen the remaining skeleton of the *Fortuna* - right up there - at 16th Street where it still lies buried several feet beneath the sand. The recovery of the *Fortuna's* anchor sparked renewed interest in its history, and the story has grown from a short paragraph in the "Lure of Long Beach" to volumes of information on the subject. And, where did all this information come from after being buried for so many years? A lot came from the only source capable of filling in the gaps - from Saveria Fortunata Marina Adragna, the daughter of the *Fortuna's* captain who was born on and rescued from the *Fortuna* when she was only six weeks old. Of course she remembered nothing of the shipwreck, only the stories her father shared with his family. And, we knew nothing of the family, only the details of the wreck as reported in our local history books. Through this friendship which stretches across the ocean thousands of miles, we are now able to piece together all the parts of the *Fortuna* story and come up with the entire, documented history, complete with living characters.

This anchor certainly does represent a magnificent treasure for Ship Bottom to display, one which symbolizes an era few of us remember, linking us more closely with our maritime past. But the real treasure lies right here - in the people who have joined together, unselfishly, to make this monument a reality...from the physical labor, the monetary contributions and the words of encouragement, through to the silent forces who sat a vigil by the anchor throughout the night so the cement could harden free from unwanted initials or footprints. We can all be proud - yes, every one of us - of the part we've played in preserving this anchor for the future. But, none would be more proud than Captain Giovan Battista Adragna himself to know that his ship was not lost in vain, and through the dedicated efforts of many, the anchor from his ship will live on in the memory of those who come to view it as a lasting tribute to the men who made their living from the sea.

Mayor Nissen, will you please come forward. It is with a touch of sadness, but also with feelings of great pride and accomplishment, that I present to you in the name of Ship Bottom, this anchor from the *Fortuna* for dedication in honor of those who sailed and lost their lives in these treacherous waters of Long Beach Island, and to the crews of the Life Saving Stations who risked their own lives in heroic efforts to save others.

Carole Bradshaw,
The Anchor Lady

September 28, 1985

I was humbled by the standing ovation I received following my speech. I think that's when it hit me that I, too, was a celebrity.

Following the ceremony, Saveria was surrounded by autograph seekers, anxious to have their programs signed by "the *Fortuna* baby" herself. Saveria proudly signed each program, adding a personal message to each. What a trooper!

By this time Giuseppe was busy inspecting the plaques surrounding the anchor and had recognized a few names from previous introductions: Toriello, Nissen, Previto, Bradshaw, The Anchor Lady were all very familiar by now. His eyes welled up with tears as he read the names of his family: his father, Captain Giovan Battista Adragna; his mother, Maria Savona Adragna; his two sisters, Antonina and Anna, complete with dates of births and deaths; and one for Saveria and himself listing only their births. He dried his eyes and rejoined the celebration.

The celebrations continued at the Ship Bottom Fire House where a luncheon sponsored by the Ship Bottom Civic Association was held for our honored guests, providing a marvelous opportunity for the people of Ship Bottom to meet the *Fortuna* baby, up close and personal. By this time, Saveria and Giuseppe were quite accustomed to being in the spotlight and didn't seem to mind that they couldn't understand anything that was being said to them.

The afternoon break from our over-scheduled day came as a chance to show Saveria and Giuseppe the things on Long Beach Island that would mean a lot to them. Our first stop, of course, was the 16th Street beach in Ship Bottom, the site of the wreck of the *Fortuna* seventy-five years before; the place where Saveria was rescued from her father's ship when she was a baby, too young to remember. It was difficult to know how Saveria felt to be standing on the beach at the very spot where the *Fortuna's* good fortune had ended. Right under their feet, buried deep beneath the sand, was the remaining skeleton of the *Fortuna*. I had shown them pictures of the ship's remains, but as they say, one picture is worth a thousand words, yet they remained speechless. From the beach, we headed south to the Little Egg Harbor Yacht Club in Beach Haven to see the mast from the *Fortuna*. Shortly after the shipwreck, the main mast was salvaged and hauled by horse-drawn wagon down the seven mile, unpaved road to the yacht club where it was erected as a flag pole. Saveria and Giuseppe were again overcome with emotion when they touched a remaining part of their father's ship. They were flooded with thoughts of their family who often spoke of their happy days aboard the *Fortuna*, and how their mother may have sat next to this mast as young Anna and Antonina played around it. All that was gone now, but for a moment, standing under the flagpole, it brought the visions back to mind. Before taking Saveria and Giuseppe back to their house, we stopped at a local shop to purchase some postcards for them to send to friends back home. Most likely, though, they were home before the cards arrived.

As the festivities of the day began to wind down, so did our energy levels. We welcomed the chance to spend a quiet dinner at home as a family; just Saveria, Giuseppe, Franco and my family. It was a special evening for all of us.

*   *   *   *   *

After such festive celebrations on Saturday, a more somber ceremony was scheduled for Sunday morning. A memorial service on the 16th Street beach in Ship Bottom was celebrated in memory of the *Fortuna*, her captain, the crew and passengers, as well as to honor the memory of the many ships and lives that were lost on our beaches. The Mass was delivered by Father Christian Camadella, pastor at St. Francis of Assisi who, like Father Whalen - who delivered the original Mass aboard the Fortuna at this exact spot in 1910 - also spoke fluent Italian.

It was a very moving service. The participation of the United States Coast Guard from the Barnegat Light Station was especially symbolic. As linear descendants of the U.S. Life Saving Service, we remembered, with gratitude, the risks they took and sacrifices they made for those imperiled on the sea. A coast guard rescue vessel laid a memorial wreath on the water off shore. At the conclusion of the ceremony, a young man swam out to retrieve the wreath and presented it to Saveria who later placed it on the head post of the anchor monument that bore the name of her father. Regretfully, Jerry Sprague, the only other living person who had once been on board the *Fortuna*, was too ill to attend the ceremony. Before leaving the beach, Saveria and Giuseppe stepped away from the crowd to spend a few moments by themselves as they reflected on their father, the *Fortuna*, and their family. They offered a silent prayer before leaving the beach.

By Monday, the celebrations were starting to wind down. Saveria and Giuseppe were due to head back home to Trapani later in the day, but there was one more public appearance scheduled for Saveria. Along with Mario as our interpreter, we went to the Long Beach Island Grade School where the children met "the rescued baby" they studied about in their history book. Some of the younger students were expecting to see a baby, while the older ones who "could do the math" knew exactly how old the baby would be by now. They were so excited to meet a living person from the pages of their history book. Saveria answered their questions through interpretation by Mario, and posed with them for many photographs. The students presented her with a card signed by each and every one of them, and Saveria presented each and every one of them with a kiss on the cheek; gifts they will remember and treasure forever.

*   *   *   *   *

It was a bittersweet moment for Giuseppe and Saveria as I drove over the causeway leaving Long Beach Island behind. The past few days had brought so much joy and importance into their lives, it was hard for them to leave. The people, the celebrations, the tributes to their father. At times it had all seemed overwhelming, yet it gave Saveria and Giuseppe the chance to look back to a time in their father's life that once had caused the family sadness. Now, with the passage of time, they could see things in a different light. Things would be different when they got back home.

Saveria and Giuseppe slept during the entire three hour ride to Kennedy Airport in New York. They were totally exhausted from all the festivities and whirl-wind of activities, but they were so happy, like children who had just received the best gift ever on Christmas morning. We arrived at the airport terminal just in time for them to present their tickets and check their luggage. I watched as the Alitalia representative escorted them down the corridor to their plane that would take them back to Trapani. I wanted so much to rush out just one more time and tell them how much we enjoyed their visit, and hug and kiss them one more time, but, of course, regulations prevented me from doing that. Darn those regulations! They can just ruin things at times.

Giuseppe called Franco at the barber shop the next day to let him know they had returned home safely and found everything okay when they arrived back in Trapani. It was quite a while before we received another letter from Saveria. When the letter did arrive, it was lengthy, and explained that she could not write sooner because every time she sat down to write she was overcome with such emotion that she could not continue. By that, I knew they had a wonderful time.

(Translated letter from Saveria)

October 7, 1985
Dear Carole,

After a marvelous return trip we are again in our Trapani in the company of Maria and her sister, Nina. They were waiting for us with trepidation and anxiety. Seeing us again was very touching for them. So deep was their desire to see us again, they missed us very much.

As soon as we stepped on the plane and we heard the roar of the motor, our hearts started to beat with particular rapidity, thinking so much of the emotion in living in the noble and hospitable land of Ship Bottom, and all of the people that during our brief stay showed us so much love, sympathy and welcome. In that moment, we would have liked to come off the airplane in order to tell you once more our very sincere thank you for the beautiful, happy days spent in your company.

We would like to send to you a very particular thank you for all the manifestations in honor of our father and his ship, *Fortuna*. Through the monument, memories will be projected into the future. But, in leaving Ship Bottom, we were taken by the nostalgia of our dear Carole to whom we feel tied by an unbreakable friendship and gratitude for taking the initiative for the finished product, and for allowing us to realize a dream we thought was almost impossible. Through you, we would like to express our thanks and appreciation to the Mayor and his wife, the family of Mr. Toriello, and to Franco Di Gangi, and also to everyone who welcomed us with so much love. In time we will thank them personally, as soon as we recuperate from the emotion and stress of this trip to Ship Bottom.

Recently I visited the Sanctuary of the Madonna of Trapani for thanksgiving in surviving the hurricane and prayed in the name of all the people of Ship Bottom.

I send all my best wishes, and from my brother, Giuseppe, to all our friends there, especially Mayor, Mr. Toriello, Franco and their families. From our heart, receive united wishes to your family. We send kisses and embraces, particularly to the little Jonathan. Many regards from Maria, and she thanks you for the beautiful music box. She will think of you whenever she hears its tune.

Marina and Giuseppe

We arranged for a video tape of the dedication ceremony to be forwarded to Saveria and Giuseppe so they could show all their friends the celebrations held in their honor when they were in Ship Bottom. It didn't really matter that it was in English; they could be their own translators.

Back in their apartment in Trapani, over the mantle in their living room where once just the photos of their mother and father hung side by side, there are now other mementos, just as precious, hanging alongside them: a photograph of their dear Carole, a photograph of the *Fortuna* anchor monument, and a letter addressed to them from President Ronald Reagan.

Not long after Saveria and Giuseppe had returned home to Trapani, I received another letter from Saveria telling how they had been interviewed for a television program to be aired in all of Sicily, not just in their city of Trapani. She included an article and photograph that was published in the Sicilian Journal. Saveria wrote how, after the article was published, every time she and Giuseppe walked the streets, people would stop them and ask questions about the story. And several friends with whom they had lost contact, called to say they read about them, or saw them on television. Now, back in their own hometown, they were celebrities just like they had been when they visited Ship Bottom, and they were enjoying every minute of it. How very different it was from the years when Saveria and Giuseppe were growing up and the wreck of the *Fortuna* was something they could never mention. After their father had been honored by the town of Ship Bottom and praised for his heroic actions by the President of the United States, Saveria and Giuseppe could remove the black cloud that had hung over their heads for so long and speak openly and proudly of their loving father, the dedicated Captaino, the Master of the *Fortuna*.

Saveria and Franco Di Gangi listen to dedication speech.

Mayor Robert Nissen holds anchor dedication plaque.

Greg Bradshaw, Saveria, Carole Bradshaw, Giuseppe

Giuseppe and Saveria enjoy a moment at the dedication ceremony.

THE WHITE HOUSE

WASHINGTON

September 23, 1985

I am very pleased to send greetings to everyone
taking part in the dedication of the anchor from the
square-rigger FORTUNA. My particular welcome goes
to Signorina Saveria Fortunata Marina Adragna, the
only surviving passenger of the wreck of the
FORTUNA, and her brother Giuseppe.

The anchor will serve as a reminder of a dramatic event
in your community's history. You can take special
pride in the fact that so many citizens banded together
and raised the funds themselves to mount the anchor in
a suitable setting. Your actions demonstrate the kind
of community spirit that has done so much to make this
country a wonderful place to live.

Nancy joins me in sending best wishes to all for a
memorable day. God bless you.

Ronald Reagan

Saveria and Giuseppe
stand on the beach
where the remains
of their father's ship,
Fortuna, are beneath
their feet.

The skeleton of the
Fortuna became
visible after severe
beach erosion in
April 1983.

Shipwrecks are the most exaggerated stories of all maritime subjects. With every repetition, the level of heroism attached to the shipwreck grows.

January 14, 1986

The following is a translation of an article published in the <u>"Sicilian Chronicle"</u> (Italy) several months after the dedication ceremony:

"Captain Saved All Survivors. Daughter of Captain Adragna, National Hero of Ship Bottom, Came Back From U.S. She Received Letter from Reagan"

TRAPANI. Once upon a time there was a boat that in one night during a very serious storm was swallowed by the waves. All the crew was saved with the help of a courageous captain of the ship after three days of agony, leaning on one side, and nothing was left. After many years, this enchanted sailboat resurfaced from the sand that buried it. From the anchor it was possible to get the name of the ship. The story that came out tells us the adventure of a little fortunate girl, and the story of an expert seaman who for the local people has become a hero. This fantastic, modern story with a happy ending wouldn't have been possible to surface if an American archaeologist didn't dedicate three years of her life to putting together the pieces of this fascinating puzzle of the lives of these real life people. The only one still alive is Saveria Fortunata Marina Adragna. She is seventy-six years old and lives in Trapani together with her brother. The daughter is of Captain Giovan Battista Adragna, an old sailor that New Jersey has proclaimed as a national hero choosing his boat as a symbol of the Community of Ship Bottom (city of approximately 200,000 inhabitants) facing the Atlantic Ocean.

Captain Adragna was in charge of the boat when on the night of January 19, 1910 a violent hurricane forced the boat to lean on the side producing a hole that forced it to be beached. All this happened on the beach of Ship Bottom. The boat was made of metal and had three sail-masts. It was headed for New York with a cargo of French tiles. On the boat there were the Captain Giovan Battista Adragna, 38 years old, from Trapani, 13 men as a crew, his wife that went along on the trip as a "stowaway of love" and the daughter Marina born on the ship three days before the shipwreck.

The *Fortuna* sank and the lifeboat saved everybody. It was a happy ending also for the baby for, in the middle of flames, a sailor put her into a burlap sack which he tied to a float and threw it overboard. The very sharp sight of a crew member saw her being thrown overboard, and was able to calculate the projectory-fall of this strange object and intercept it in the water and by swimming, brought it to the beach. The baby was soaking wet, but was saved and looked well. Meanwhile, Captain Adragna continued the operation of saving the crew with courage, even without forgetting the little animals that were aboard. He was the last one to get off the ship and remain safely on the beach.

At the end everybody was lucky and people of the community were happy because for the first time after 150 tragic shipwrecks, the entire crew of a boat was saved. And so, the story ended and the Adragnas went back to Trapani. The Adragnas swore to themselves never to tell the children about that tragic night.

On March 13, 1983 at Ship Bottom, an archaeologist, Carole Bradshaw, noticed that a severe thunderstorm the preceding day uncovered an antique relic that was protruding from the sand. She noticed an inscription on it: the word *FORTUNA*. In that finding, Carole saw a sign of the destiny that gave her the opportunity to settle the argument that was growing in the city of Ship Bottom over the symbol to be chosen as the official insignia to be given to the town in the occasion of their 60th Anniversary of its founding. The borough, with the help of the Governor of New Jersey, approved the program that Carole submitted for the reconstruction of the history of the boat, *Fortuna*. After three years of research in the U.S. and Italy, all was known about the boat from Trapani. She was able to complete the puzzle because of the precious testimony that Captain Adragna gave immediately after the wreck to New York Harbor authorities. All this story was told as a novel without missing the smallest detail. The population of Ship Bottom (at this point was 200,000) was taken by this fascinating story and it was now indispensible to find Marina, the baby saved by a miracle from death.

She was found and last December Miss Adragna, now 76 years old, with Giuseppe went to America. In Ship Bottom, besides finding a piece of history she never knew, Marina had the pleasant surprise to find her father's pictures everywhere. Giant photos of the captain could be found on streets, on signs, affixed to buildings and on shirts, different gadgets, in school books for students, and police cars In short, the *Fortuna* and captain are the symbol of the city.

Saveria Marina uncovered the monument in honor of her father and she dedicated schools named after her father, Captain Adragna. She participated in the presentation of a book on the Captain from Trapani. A publishing house has prepared a series of photo-cards entitled "The Adventures of Captain Adragna," and a T.V. station, a subsidiary of ABC, has aired a documentary that was viewed by all in New Jersey. They are already involved in the making of a movie. All the most important American newspapers dedicated space to articles around this fairy tale with a happy ending. After 10 days of celebrating, we felt like royalty. Saveria and Giuseppe are now back in Trapani. Once in a while we pinch ourselves to verify that this was not a dream, but after we look at the beautiful gifts the Americans gave to us and touch the letter President Reagan wrote to us, we realize it all really happened.

This shows that life is always coming up with surprises!

Giacomo Pilati, Cronache Siciliane

*   *   *   *   *

Epilogue: November 2009

For many years, I continued to walk along the beaches of Long Beach Island looking for treasures. Well, to be truthful, I was just hoping to find more red *Fortuna* tiles. But, I didn't find many. I had a theory, though. After giving so many presentations about the anchor, lots of beachcombers had learned what those red tiles were. Instead of walking by them like they used to, now they are collecting them as valuable treasures.

A long time has passed since Alison and I first walked on the beach to collect our treasures. She's all grown up now, but I remember those days as if they were just yesterday. Just recently, I was sitting on the beach and watched as a young mother walked along the edge of the water with her small daughter in hand. I chuckled to myself as the young girl ran ahead in excitement to pick up a piece of green sea glass before it vanished in the surf. It brought back fond memories as I watched them put their treasure in the little red pail. Just a few moments after they passed by, I caught a glimpse of something red being tossed around in the surf. Could it be? I quickly got out of my chair and rushed towards the object, but by the time I got there, it was gone. I wondered - was it another piece of red tile from the *Fortuna*? Most likely, it was. But I'll never know for sure.

The last letter I received from Saveria was dated October 1989.

APPENDICES

I. Personal correspondence

Caldwell, New Jersey
June 29, 1984

Dear Carole,

WE DID IT!

I have just received a letter from the town of Trapani (from the mayor). They have found one son of the Captain Adragna. Here are the details:

Captain Adragna Giovan Battista of Giuseppe (his father) and of Trapani Antonina (his mother) born in Trapani 1/1/1867 and passed away in Trapani 6/3/1954. Now the son!

Adragna Giuseppe (son of Captain Adragna) born in Trapani 5/4/1912 and living in Trapani at Via Delle Acacie No. 27.

So, CONGRATULATIONS!

Franco

#

July 5, 1984

Dear Franco,

I can tell by your letter that you were excited to receive a reply from Trapani! Well, I was, too. I can't tell you how much this means!! Sorry to say for you it means more letter-translating, but... we've gotten this far; we have to do more!

I was happy to learn that the Captain did not commit suicide as reported in the American newspapers. He died a natural death at 87 in 1954. Also, now we can contact the son and get more information.

Enclosed is a letter I would like to send to the son. I have also enclosed a copy of our original letter so we won't have to explain it all over again. Money is enclosed for postage and a stamped address envelope for you to mail out the letter after you've translated it into Italian. I would appreciate it if you would save the letters you receive, for I'd like to keep a complete file.

This son was not listed in the phone book of names we got from the Consulate. So, we never would have found him if we had not heard from the mayor. Good work!

Thanks a lot,
Carole

#

July 5, 1984
Giuseppe Adragna
Trapani, Sicily

Dear Mr. Adragna,

I have been searching for a child of Captain G.B. Adragna, Master of the *Fortuna* at the time of its loss in 1910. Your name has been sent to me, and I am hoping that you are, indeed, Captain Giovan's son.

Please read the enclosed letter. It will explain why I am doing this research and why it is important for you to contact me.

We know a lot about the circumstances of the shipwreck, but very little about the captain's life... his family, his career, what he was like as a person. Also, any stories he might have told about the wreck of the *Fortuna* in America.

It was reported that his wife and three children (one a newborn baby) were rescued from the ship. Are any of these children still living? If so, where can I write to them? Also, a photograph of the captain or wife and children would be very desirable. We would like to know as much as possible about the people associated with the captain and *Fortuna*. If you have a photograph, I can duplicate it and return your original.

I would appreciate it if you would verify that you are his son. Upon your reply, I will share information I have about the *Fortuna's* history and photographs which I have obtained. We are an Island town, so very much smaller than your Island of Sicily, but your father's ship was a very important part of our history.

Hoping to hear from you very soon.
Franco Di Gangi (for Carole Bradshaw)

\#

August 22, 1984

Dear Saveria Adragna,

My name is Carole Bradshaw, and I was the one who found the anchor to your father's ship, and the one who has been searching for you. Mr. Franco Di Gangi, who is a neighbor of mine, has been so kind and helpful in translating my letters to you. Without his help, we never would have found you. All correspondence should still go through him.

I am so excited to find you after so many years! It was only after I found the anchor of your father's ship that I thought it would make the story complete to find the "newborn baby" who was rescued from the *Fortuna* when it wrecked on the beach in 1910. Now that we have found you, we would certainly like to have you here for our dedication ceremonies next year.

It would be important to receive the photographs that your brother mentioned he would send me. Right now, the only photos I have are the ones taken while the Fortuna was stranded on our beach. A photo of your family, your father, and the ship would give us a chance to see what you all look like. Thank you for sending them.

I am looking forward to hearing from you. Mr. Di Gangi will continue to translate my letters to you.

I am happy to write to you - I feel that I have found a long, lost friend. Write soon.

Sincerely,
Carole Bradshaw

#

September 5, 1984

Dear Mr. Di Gangi,

Through one of my relatives (Joseph Previto) I recently received a letter from Carole Bradshaw in which she told me about an article in the newspaper that explains the importance of the project to your small city. In regard to the article, Mr. Di Gangi, I would like a translated copy. Carole said she is waiting for photographs, which I already sent. Carole was asking about the log in order to have exact information about the sinking of the *Fortuna* and of its trips before the ship was lost on your coast. I am sorry to say I cannot satisfy your request as I remember my father saying the log was lost with the *Fortuna*, and that the boat sank because of a strong storm. But I can assure you it left Marseille, France, empty and was going to Montevideo when it was forced to stop over in Barbados because Saveria was due to be born very soon. If no bother, in order to have knowledge about the plans Mrs. Carole wants to put together for the monument to my father, Mr. Di Gangi, would you tell us more about the project. I am always grateful of your kind interest and thank you very much.

Best regards,
Giuseppe and Saveria Adragna

#

October 12, 1984

Dear Mrs. Carole,

First of all, thank you for the kind thought in sending us the shirt with the insignia of the anchor of the *Fortuna*. We compliment you very much on your initiative and we hope that this project will have full success. In this way, you will see your goal realized and with the funds you are collecting, you will be able to build the monument and satisfy your wish. Besides, for us it will be a reason of pride and we will be touched knowing the person who is so good and kind, is interested in a land so far away, to remember the disaster to the ship of my father, Captain Giovan Batista Adragna. But what has touched us most, is your profound generosity and goodness. Your very gentle thought in sending us your pictures enables us to know you almost personally, dear Mrs. Carole, and the members of your family. Also, our friend, Mr. Di Gangi, and the city where the sinking of the ship occurred. The reaction of the city to your project would have touched my father's heart if he were still living. I can assure you that we cried of emotion in reading on the anchor my first and last name, and the date I was born. I had heard the circumstances of my unique birth in stories from my father. From your pictures, we are sure, as we thought, that you are a very special person and your sensitivity in wanting to honor my father's memory is surely appreciated. As you requested, we send you the signed card and in this way you can utilize it with our authorization to publish our pictures and anything you wish in the newspaper. Hope you will write to us soon with good news. Meanwhile, please accept our most sincere wishes of good health to you, to the members of your family, and our friend, Mr. Di Gangi.

Saveria & Giuseppe Adragna

#

March 23, 1985

Dear Marina and Giuseppe,

It is very difficult to write in words - even with all of Mr. Di Gangi's help - my feelings about meeting you during our trip to Trapani. After all these years of studying about the *Fortuna* and researching the wreck, to actually meet, in person, the children of Captain Adragna, creates such a feeling inside me that I cannot express in words. I have grown to admire your father greatly during the time I studied the *Fortuna*, and through meeting you, have a deeper feeling for him as a man, as a sea captain and as a father. You were exactly what I thought you would be like: very warm and loving people who welcomed us into your family with open hearts. By the time we said goodbye, which was much too soon, we felt as though we had been a part of your dear family forever.

Meeting you has been one of the most wonderful experiences of my life - one which I never will forget.

I thank you very much for all the information you shared with us about your family. I realize that there was so much that was personal to you, and I feel very honored that you were eager to share it with us. It has made us better understand the life your father had as a sea captain, and the tender role he played as a father. Your stories allowed me to appreciate the lives of your parents, and the sacrifices they made for his career. It was no doubt hard for your father and mother to separate when he went to sea for so long. The fact that she followed him to Marseille to accompany him on his last voyage of the *Fortuna* showed real love and devotion. The "raising of the flags when his 'son' was born in Barbados" lets us know how much he truly loved each of his children.

Also, thank you for taking us to the cemetery where I could be with the spirit of your father. It was a very moving moment for me, for it was through him that we were able to be brought together from two lands so far apart.

Giuseppe, I especially want to thank you for taking so much time from your own family to show us the many interesting sights around Trapani. I am very sorry that your wife, Maria, could not have shared more in our visit. She is such a sweet person, and her love and warmth showed through on her face. She is fortunate to have such a caring and wonderful family to care for her needs. You do have a very special family.

My telephone rings constantly with people asking what the "baby" looks like, and can't wait to share the pictures. All our books, including the school's local history book, just know you, Marina, as the "newly born baby who was rescued from the ship." So you can imagine how excited we all are to show a present day photo of you. I am mailing some pictures of our trip so you can share in the reminder of our good times. I love these pictures so much that I will hang them on the wall with those of the rest of my family.

Until recently I had never heard of Trapani. Then it became a town with a name. But, now I have been there and love it. I enjoyed learning a bit about where you live and seeing the many things which make your town special. With all the new pictures I have to add to my anchor presentations and the *Fortuna* history, we will be able to raise all the money needed to complete the anchor monument. You would really be proud of it, but the best part would be to be here in September to see it and be part of dedicating it to our town in your father's honor. We are looking forward to that moment very much.

I am so glad I walked on the beach last year and found the *Fortuna* anchor, because that has made it possible to locate you, and I would not have missed that chance for the world. It is hard to express through someone else's words what it has meant to me, but after knowing you for such a short time, I feel as though I have known you forever. It was so hard saying goodbye at the airport, and I was trying to hold back the tears of sadness because I knew if I started to cry, we would all be in tears within moments. But, we do have our next meeting to look forward to and that will be a joyous time for us all.

I know I will never get to the point where we can converse together in the same language, but as I continue to study, maybe by September we can express a lot more. Although, Franco says I will never learn to speak Italian!

With lots of love,
Carole and Greg

#

April 27, 1985

Dear Carole and Gregory,

We received with great happiness your letter and pictures you took while you were here in Trapani. While looking at them we relived for a moment, the beautiful time we spent together in those short but very intense days. Giuseppe and I are very happy to have had the opportunity to meet the person so exquisite and kind, and such people who give so much of themselves. Believe us when we say that nobody could be as kind as you are. What we did for you while you were here we did with all of our heart for you and the memory of our father. As you have written, he was a good captain, a good father, and a marvelously courageous man.

Regarding the pictures, we already distributed them to the young man at the florist, and to our friend, Turiddu, and we assure you, they thank you very much and send their sincere appreciation.

I am very happy that you're wearing my very modest present and am also touched about your kind expression which sounded like it came from the heart of an old friend. We are also happy the children liked our sweets, and please give a big kiss to them as if we were there.

We are sure that when we come to visit you there, we would receive a bigger welcome than we were able to give you when you came to visit us in Trapani. We are very anxious to see the monument to our father, the man we loved so very much both when he was alive, and after his death. We are at the same time, proud of him, and because through your help and initiative, he has left an imprint of his existence for the future. This mater, believe me, touches our heart, and we are longing for the commemoration. We, too, were very touched the day you left because we didn't think there could exist people like you who do so much for others. This kind of pessimism with human nature is due to the world full of much evil and that there are few persons still able to do so much good - and you are part of that last category.

When we see you again, dear Carole, I am sure you would speak Italian fluently. We won't be able to speak your language because of our age it would be too difficult. I'm sure you will understand.

We embrace and send regards to your children, and hope to know them soon. We send regards to Mr. Di Gangi and his family, and look forward to meeting them soon.

Marina and Giuseppe

#

February 3, 1986

Dear Carole,

We refer to your letter of last January and we are more than happy to give you our full cooperation in sending you the necessary news you requested. We appreciate your tremendous devotion to accomplish the task of writing a book which will be beneficial to our family and the achievements of our father. It certainly would be a book which will highlight once more your great feelings and interest in human nature, your goodness and spirit of sacrifice and your excellent gift to organize, but certainly it will show how you, our dear Carole, after having immortalized the memory of our father by the construction of a monument in a land so far away, and now through your book, will propagate the heroism to a vast number of people.

Our father has two brothers, Vito and Antonino (both sea captains) and one sister, Saveria.

The father of our father was named Giuseppe (he was also a sea captain)

Our father married when he was thirty three years old, and our mother, Maria Savona, was twenty years old. We do not know how they met, but we are sure that it was a marriage of love, and they spent their life in harmony and love.

We are not able to tell you when my father became partners in the ownership of the *Fortuna*. We only know that the three owners were: Giovan Battista Adragna (our father) Captain Baldassare Savona, brother of our mother, and Aloisio Salvatore, father in law of Baldessare Savona.

Our father, in charge of the *Fortuna*, sailed from Trapani in the month of January 1909, bound for France where he docked in the harbor of Marseille. It was here that my mother, in the company of her two daughters Antonina and Anna, met him and decided to go with him.

We hope that we have been helpful to you, and we wish you all the luck in the world and a great success in finishing the big project that you undertook. We think of you all the time and, again, we are very grateful to you.

Marina and Giuseppe

#

April 21, 1986

Dear Carole,

We are sorry for the delay in answering your letter. Our intentions to write were sincere, but Maria was not feeling too well. Her condition is getting worse, forcing us to give her more attention during the day and also the night. We admit that we are very tired, and besides the energy required to care for her, we also have deep preoccupation with her health.

But now we find ourselves with peace and a period of tranquility and we write to you, our good and dear Carole that deserves all our intense attention and gratitude for all you have done. We thank you very much from the bottom of our hearts for the pictures that you kindly sent to us, but most of all, we would like to thank you again for the interest and work that you are taking in writing the book on the story of the *Fortuna*, and about all that our father did. In order to help you, we send you the information that you requested.

Giuseppe grew up in the midst of our family and received a very strict education, moral and religious. He went to high school, and when he was going to work, he was called into the army for the draft, and consequently he was sent to Abyssinia (in Africa) since at the time, Italy declared war on such a nation in 1939. We were almost ready to recuperate from this war, but in 1940 World war broke out again and Giuseppe was forced to stay in the service, and he was sent to the front where there was fighting and he was taken prisoner from the English. In 1940 he was sent to the concentration camp in Kenya, and then from there he was transferred to London where he was liberated at the end of World War II. Finally in 1946, he came back to the midst of our family. Once the war was over, Giuseppe came back to Trapani where he was employed as a technical operator in the Civil Hospital of Trapani. He worked there until he reached the age of retirement in 1972.

Receive our affectionate embraces from Maria, Giuseppe and Nina.

Marina and Giuseppe

#

May 2, 1986

Dear Carole,

The deep expression of love and friendship that we write to you in our letters to you are really felt sincerely from the bottom of our hearts. How can we not admire and love you because you have been a tireless worker on all the manifestations in honor of our father and the story of the boat, *Fortuna*, that all happened because of your sincere interest. How can we ever forget that without your initiative and constant work and dedication, all this would have been forgotten forever, and we are firm believers that even today, the anchor would still be at the bottom of the sea and forgotten. We appreciate very much and understand your big sacrifice to go aboard a boat similar to the *Fortuna* for the reason to understand life at sea. In this way you will be able to realize your goal and be able to describe in detail the history of the *Fortuna* and of her Captain and his family with more feeling of truth and actuality.

Regarding the news you requested about Antonina and Anna, we would love to remain quiet in order not to open the big wound and pain we feel, and leave them to rest in peace. But we understand that the story you are writing has to be complete and has to be close to the truth and we decided that since we are speaking about the head of the family, it is also right that it should be spoken about the members of his family, present and absent. For this reason we are very happy to tell you the news that you requested.

Antonina was born in Trapani on February 9, 1903. She was very vivacious, loved company and was loved by all her friends. She went to high school and was a very good student. She loved music and singing, and you could hear her sing almost all day long. She went on many trips to keep company with our father. After her studies she dedicated herself with love to the house. When she was twenty three, she met a young man to whom she was going to marry, but unfortunately she could not realize this beautiful dream of love because a cruel sickness took her when she was only twenty seven years old.

Anna was born in Trapani on January 16, 1907. She was very bright, quiet and shy. She did not want to go traveling with my father and preferred to stay near her mother to whom she felt a very deep affection.

She went to Junior High School, and she died an early death when she was only fourteen years old.

Yours always,
Marina and Giuseppe

#

May 30, 1986

Dear Carole and Family,

Excuse me if we were late in writing back to you. The lateness is due to the condition of Maria which is very serious. We confess that we are really worried and because of that, time flies and we do not realize how quickly the weeks go by. We hope that God will give us the strength to live through this tremendous crisis.

We are generally feeling pretty good and we hope that you and your family are in good health. I am sending you a picture to remind you again of your dear Marina who will never forget you. Your very affectionate letters which touch my heart both for your beautiful expression of goodness and love that makes us feel like we belong to the same family, and for the sincere and genuine feelings of fraternity that unite us as members of one big family. We always think about you as if I were a mother who lives far away who always thinks about her own children. Dear Carole, I send you my most dear thoughts and kisses. When Giuseppe received your gift for his birthday he was so very, very touched by your kind thoughts, and he started to cry.

With love and affection,
Marina

#

May 30, 1986

Dear Carole,

On the occasion of my birthday I received your beautiful gift of a silver dollar. I admire your thoughts and it gives me so much happiness, not for the gift, but because it was the sign of a complete and truly sincere friendship that you never forget any occasion to show us that your thoughts and understanding is always in our direction. I will save with particular care the gift which will give me the occasion when I look at it to think of you and all of my friends in Ship Bottom. Again, I thank you with all my heart and affectionate embrace.

With all my love,
Giuseppe

#

March 1987

Dear Carole,

Although I am deeply troubled and emotionally down I wish to find a moment of relaxation to write to you. Just a moment of quiet thoughts of you helps to diminish my pain. I know our friend Franco Di Gangi has already told you of the sudden death of my brother, Giuseppe, that happened February 21, 1987. The tragedy that became upon my family is more painful because it was a loss that we did not expect and has left us numb for the way it happened. Now I feel alone and when I go from room to room it seems to me that I see the big statue of my brother, and I think I hear his words and what he says to me in a joking way. I remember Giuseppe with a great pain, but a lot of love; love that is shared by his friends that loved him for his good humor, for his understanding, for his concern about everybody and he never lacked a desire to help his friends. I hope I am not presumptuous in exalting the virtues of my brother because even you, in his short stay in your land, had the opportunity to appreciate him for his goodness and for his will to help everybody. My pain is diminishing because I think of the beautiful gifts, both moral and religious, Giuseppe will receive from God - a grace of eternal life, and he will rest in peace. I am sorry to disturb you but am sure you will consider the state in which I am in. At this moment I wish I could have received a letter from you which would show a moment of solidarity and affection that would have brought a spiritual calm to my soul to hear a word of comfort from you, but unfortunately, we are so far away that it is necessary for me to wait. I will remember you always with affection and gratitude and finish sending you my kisses and best regards to you and your family.

With affection,
Marina

#

March 13, 1987

Dear Marina,

There are not many words I can write to express our deepest sympathy for the loss of your dear brother, Giuseppe. We feel the same sadness you feel, and we will miss him greatly. We feel blessed that we had the chance to meet him and to know him, briefly. Giuseppe touched our hearts with so much goodness and kindness. We truly felt like he was part of our family.

I would like for you to have this rosary as a special gift to you, in memory of Giuseppe. Please use it to pray for his soul; that his spirit may live on in all of us. God bless him and comfort you at this time.

Our entire family joins together in wishing you good health and the strength to carry on. God bless you, Marina. You are always in our thoughts and prayers. We love you and will keep in touch very often.

With much love and deep affection,
Carole, Greg and family

#

April 4, 1987

Dear Carole,

I just received the package that you sent to me with the holy rosary, and it was really beautiful. I do not have the words to express to you my true feelings of gratitude. Many thanks especially for the deep spiritual meaning of your religious gift. I guarantee that I will use it to honor Giuseppe's memory and also to bring peace to his soul through my prayers because God has given him eternal rest, and he has been taken in with all the saints. The beautiful gift was accompanied by a beautiful letter with a very touching expression of love, and I confess that I cried. Dear Carole, again, thank you for the way in which you wanted to remember Giuseppe; for his goodness and kindness, his human sensitivity and his good heart. Thank you again for the beautiful expression to wish me to be strong and in the future, I will remember what you say. But for the moment, I am deeply in pain and I meditate the situation in which I find myself. When Giuseppe died, he created around me a very serious emptiness and also with his death, it took some of myself. My heart cries every day for his loss, and I am sure that all this requires a certain period of time before I feel like myself. In the meantime, I will accept words of comfort from people who really love me and from people who look to give me strength and tranquility. That will offer some kind of remedy to my continued state of tension. Thanks again for your love, my dear Carole, and your kind thoughts, and also because you say you pray for me. I send you all my love, and to your family and also thank them for the rosary.

I embrace you with all my heart and I will remember you forever.

Affectionately,
Marina

#

April 24, 1987

Dear Marina,

A few days ago I received your warm and touching letter in which you told me you received the rosary. I can tell from your letter that you are still grieving over the great loss of Giuseppe. You can take comfort in knowing that you are still in our prayers and though we are so far apart, and the letters take so much time to reach you, we do think of you very often, as we do our own family. I wish we could be closer in person, but you are very close now in our heart.

I thank you so much for the beautiful picture of Giuseppe. This picture will help me always remember Giuseppe with kindness, love and affection, and bring back the memories we shared on your brief visit to Ship Bottom.

You are always in our prayers and in our daily thoughts. Even as I go on with my plans to get ready for my sailing voyage, I think of you. If it were not for your father's ship, I would not be taking this sail at all. But, since the anchor has sparked my interest and made it necessary to partake in a sail before being able to write a book about it, I am entering the wonderful world of a "sailor" and enjoying every bit of it. I know I will find the voyage to be a very trying one, where I will be tired, cold, lonely, probably a bit scared, too. But, I imagine that was a bit like what it felt for your mother on her first voyage, too. So it is all connected together, and all because of you and your father's *Fortuna*, I am doing these fascinating and adventurous things.

You will forever be dear to us. Soon we will come together in person. But, for the meantime, take strength in knowing that you are close in my heart and we pray to God to keep you well. A letter never can express all the feelings we feel; I feel like I have known you all my life.

With all my love and deep affection - you are truly a wonderful person.

Carole

#

II. Official Documents and Letters

November 7, 1983

National Archives
Washington, DC 20408

Dear Sirs:

I am doing research on the Fortuna, an Italian ship that sailed and sank off the coast of Long Beach Island, New Jersey, in 1910. I am particularly interested in tracing the list of passengers on that ship. The information I already have includes:

Ship: The Fortuna - Net 924 tons
Signal Letters: PHGT
Owned by: Savona, B.
Number in Lloyd's Register of Ships Wrecked:
204 *Fortuna* - 924 tons - Ital. Iron Bark
Montevideo, via Barbados - New York
Sailed 1909 from Port of Trapani, Sicily
Sank Jan. 19, 1910 Ship Bottom NJ USA

Do you have a manifest of those aboard? The name of the ship's captain was G.B. Adragna. I am trying to find the name of the newborn baby who was on board when the ship sank.

If you can help me in any way, I would appreciate the information you can provide.

Do you also have, or know where I can obtain, an accounting of the ship's loss? I'm certain it was a news item back then and a report of it must be available somewhere.

Thank you for any information and help you can be, and I appreciate the time you put into this endeavor.

Sincerely,
Carole Bradshaw

#

National Archives and Records Service
Washington, DC 20408
Ms. Carole Bradshaw

   Records of the U.S. Coast Guard show that assistance was given to the Fortuna by the crews of the Life-Saving Stations at Ship Bottom, Harvey Cedars, and Long Beach. Each of these three stations filed a three-page report on its rescue operations. All three list the names of the seventeen persons on board, none of whom lost their lives. The first listing on all three lists of names is the Captain, "his wife and three children." The names of the wife and three children are not shown in our records, nor is there any other listing of "children" on the ship. We can furnish a copy of all three reports for our minimum fee noted above [$5.00]. Please send a check or money order payable to the National Archives Trust Fund to the cashier, National Archives (GSA), Washington, D.C. 20408

   William F. Sherman
   Judicial, Fiscal, and Social Branch
   Civil Archives Division

#

Fortuna Wreck Report Filed by the Ship Bottom Life Saving Station

Ship Bottom, Long Beach Life-Saving Station, Fifth District. (Harvey Cedars)

Date of Disaster - January 18, 1910

Name of vessel: It. Bk – *Fortuna*

Rig. Tonnage, and official number – Barque Rig ton 924

Hailing port and nationality – Trapani, Italy

Age -40

Name of Master – G.B. Adragna

Name of Owners – Adragna and others

Where from – Barbados

Where Bound – New York

Number of crew, including captain – 13 men including captain

Number of passengers - 4: captain wife, 3 children

Nature of cargo – balies [ballast]

Estimated value of vessel - $8,000

Estimated value of cargo – none

Exact place where wrecked – ½ mile north of Ship Bottom Station

Direction and distance from station – ½ mile N.E. from station

Supposed cause of disaster, (specifying particularly) – hazey weather

Nature of disaster, whether stranded, sunk, collided, etc. – stranded

Distance of vessel from shore at time of disaster – 3 hundred yards from shore

Time of day or night – 2:45 a.m.

State of wind, weather, and temperature – Wind south, weather storming

State of tide and sea – Ebb tide. High sea.

Time of discovery of wreck – 2:45 a.m.

By whom discovered – J Horace Cranmer, Abram B. Salmons

Time of starting to scene of disaster – 3:15 a.m.

Time of arrival on scene of disaster – 4:35 a.m.

Time of return to station from scene of disaster – 3:30 p.m.

Amount of damage to vessel (if totally lost, so state). – totally lost – sold for junk

Estimated value of cargo saved, and its condition – cargo, none

Amount of insurance on vessel – none

Amount of insurance on cargo – none

Number of lives saved, with names and residence – 17 – all from Trapani, Sicily, Italy

Cpt. G.B. Adragna, wife, 3 children

Mate, Michel Barbera

Giusepe Gigante

Angelo Teriste

Giuseppe Maltise

Vincenzo Papa

Francesco Rizzo

Raffaele Gigante

Michele Rallo

Giuseppe Ernancez

Salvatore Santonoberto

Francesco Pelligrio

Giuseppe Fazio

Raffalle Gigante

32. Number of lives lost – none

33. Number of persons sheltered at station, how long, and total number of meals

Furnished – 17 persons, 8 days each 17 x 136

34. Number and names of persons resuscitated from apparent death by drowning or

    Exposure to cold – none

35. Number of persons found after death and cared for – none

36. State what assistance, if any, was afforded station crew by outside parties – none

37. Who, if any, of station crew did not participate in rescue or relief work – none.

    All of station crew did partake in rescue or relief work.

USE OF BOATS AND APPARATUS

Whip line, but it got fouled. No breeches buoy used

Life boat, 3 trips, all 17 landed by boat

38. Time of launching boat – 6:00 a.m.

39. Was Lyle gun, Hunt gun, or rocket used – Yes, Lyle gun

40. Charge of powder used – 6 ounces

41. Size of shot line used – No. 9

42. Distance of wreck from shore when shot was fired – 3 hundred yards

43. Number of shots fired – 2 shots

44. If any shots were unsuccessful, state cause of failure in each case – first shot unsuccessful. Did not reach vessel.

45. Was whip line sent on board double or single – whip line sent on board double

46. If anything occurred to interfere with favorable operations, state fully nature and cause – chain on end of yard fouled. Whip line would not render in block

47. Was heaving stick used – no

48. State damage, if any t boat or apparatus – none

REMARKS:

Here should be set forth in detail the circumstances of the disaster and the measures taken to afford assistance or effect a rescue. Full information regarding each loss of life should in all cases be given. The names of all persons who volunteer, or are called upon to assist the life-saving crew in the performance of wreck or relief work should be stated. If it is necessary to hire draft animals or vehicles to transport boats or apparatus to facilitate life-saving operations that fact should be noted, and the name of the person from whom team or vehicle is hired should be mentioned.

Fired 2 shot. First shot did not reach barque. Fell short of vessel. Was farther off shore than expected. 20 elevation but shot did not reach vessel. At once hauled in shot and reloaded and shot 24 elevation. Reached the vessel. They hauled whip line on board. double. They made it fast. Foul of four yard and the chane on end of yard fouled. Whip line and whip wood not render in whip block so at day light, sea high, courant very strong, I launched surf boat and went onboard. Found it to be the barque <u>Fortuna</u> from Barbados for New York in balest. Capt. And crew all told 13 men and captains wife and 3 children. They did not want to come to shore and leave the vessel. But ask for steamboat to hall the vessel off. So I came ashore and left two of my surfmen on board to clear the whip line and have it so I cold use it if needed and went to station and sent for Meriet & Chapman Wrecking Co. And went back to barque. The tide raised and vessel came broadside on the beach and ware roling so bad the people on board wanted to come ashore. At once we launched the surfboat and 2 trips wear made with surfboat and landed all on board and brought them to station ware thay were cared for and cept warme and fed and cared for. The capt. And crew of Long Beach Station, and Capt and crew of Harvey Cedars assisted at shipwreck. At ten P.M. 22 day of January the barque roled over on her beamed end and sea weare washing her. That got ashore with the help of my crew all thay could and brought down to station ware thay could ship it to New York. The crew of barque left for New York January 26th, 1910. The vessel ware sold January 26, 1910 to parties that live in Tuckerton, N.J.

Date of report: January 27, 1910
Isaac W. Truex, Keeper

Remarks by Long Beach Life-Saving Station:

Capt. Truex called up the station on the telephone and reported ship ashore. The crew and myself got ready as soon as possible and went to there assistance. When we arrived at wreck Capt. Truex had whip line aboard but it would not work. A chain on the end of the yard fouled the whip so it would not render in the block and could not send hawser off to ship. I took part of the men and went to the station and got the boat. As soon as it was light enough we launched boat. Capt. Truex went on board of ship, got some messages to send to new york left two men on board Horace Cranmer Surfman No. 1 and William Austin Surfman No. 4 to clear whip line and see that the breeches buoy was put up right in case we could not get them in the boat so we could take them off if they would leave ship when we was along side. Hey refused to leave vessel but we took them off later in the morning in boat.
Geo. Mathis, Keeper   Jan 27th, 1910

Remarks by Harvey Cedars Life-Saving Station:

Jan. 18, 3:40 a.m. rec. tele call from Ship Bottom Sta. requesting the assistance of this crew at wreck. Keeper being absent on 24 hour liberty, #1 surfman Martin, actg. Keeper immediately responded. Starting with crew from sta. about 3:00 a.m. arrived at wreck about 5: a.m. Immediately engaged to assist in the wreck under the supervision of keeper Truex of Ship Bottom. On account of the whipline getting foul on wreck, were compelled to suspend rescue with the breeches buoy and get surfboat ready. 6:00 a.m. launched surfboat. Landed wreck.

Crew refused to leave, returned to shore for Keeper Truex to report. Leaving two surfmen on wreck to clear whipline and assist to operate the breeches buoy if necessary. About 11:00 a.m. when flood tide made they became frightened and anxious to come ashore. 11:40 a.m. Keeper of Harvey Cedars arrived to wreck in time to assist in landing crew in the surfboat in charge of Keeper Truex. 1:30 p.m. when crew were all landed, Keeper Truex informed me that nothing further could be done at present and returned to station about 3 p.m. Jan 22, about 3 a.m. wreck heeled over off shore well down on her beam ends. Indications are that she will be a total loss.
Falkenburg Jan 25, 1910

#

September 26, 1983

Mr. Robert Nissen, Mayor
17th Street
Ship Bottom, New Jersey 08008

Dear Mayor Nissen:
Congratulations to the town of Ship Bottom! **Not** because you have the anchor of the *Fortuna* to proudly place on the lawn of Borough Hall for everyone to see. **Not** because of the many anchors on this island, this is the one that has a known origin and historic past important to Long Beach Island. **Not** because we managed to salvage the anchor, which was a real accomplishment within itself. But, especially because, without the spirit of unity, determination and a sense of pride in Ship Bottom, none of the above could have been accomplished. The anchor is a real treasure for Ship Bottom, but it's the people who contributed their energies to raise the anchor that are the real prize.

I'd like to thank you and your Council for supporting my efforts on this project in July. I am sure it was a bit of a concern and worry, and a lot of wondering "if." I had hoped it would not be a disappointment - and I can see that it was not!

This winter when I'm out strolling on the beach again, would you prefer that I move on to Surf City? One project like this in Ship Bottom might be enough to last a long time!

Sincerely,
Carole Bradshaw,
The Anchor Lady

#

27 November, 1984 - from Hans Merkel

(Translation)

Ship: bark

Built: 1869

By: Reiherstieg-Werft (was bought by Deutsche-Werft in 1927)

Length 56,40m

Width: 10,10 m

Hull Height: 6,36m

Tonnage: 892 t

Carried commercial weight of 446 t

The ship was built for Reederei M. Arnesen and was sold to Reederei Pflugk verkauft in 1874

The first captain of the ship was Kapitan M. Danschow

January 1, 1985

Dear Wolfgang Loh, (friend of Eleanor Smith)
    I am very pleased and grateful for the information you sent to Axel Krueger regarding the German-built ship, Fortuna. Through various

contacts, mostly friends of friends, I have acquired much information which has never before been published about such a famous shipwreck here on the Atlantic Coast of New Jersey. It is my intention to write and publish a book about my adventure with the *Fortuna* when all the events are concluded.

This ship, the Fortuna, was lost here on our shores of New Jersey in 1910 during a terrible winter storm. All were safely rescued from the stricken ship, including a newly born baby. Through much searching and letter writing, I have located this newborn baby (now 74 years old) still living in her original town of Trapani, Sicily. I am planning to go to Trapani soon to meet her. The anchor from this ship, which weighs in the area of 8,000 lbs., was retrieved from the ocean by a group of dedicated friends last September. It will become a monument to our maritime heritage in September of 1985, the 75th anniversary of the loss of the ship.

Again thank you for all the efforts you have put into the research to help our project become a success. I was lacking the important beginnings of this ship, and you have filled in the missing pieces. I am very appreciative.

Sincerely,
Carole Bradshaw

#

August 15, 1985

President Ronald Reagan
The White House
Washington,D.C.

Dear Mr. President,

America is unique; each section, each city, each town is rich with its own history which, in the overall picture, tells the story of American history.

This year our town of Ship Bottom, New Jersey, is celebrating its 60th Anniversary. While sixty years is young in the overall age of our

Country, our history was in the making long before we became an acknowledged town! As a town on the East Coast of the United States, our waters are rich with the tales of settlers, explorers and immigrants alike, but we also keep a bit of local history alive in what we call "The Lure of Long Beach Island."

Recently, volunteer forces from Ship Bottom recovered a 116 year-old anchor from the *Fortuna*, a square-rigged sailing vessel that sailed from Trapani, Sicily en route to New York when it became a shipwreck on our shores in 1910. For many years, we've heard the interesting stories of her demise; the school children study the Fortuna as part of their Social Studies program. The discovery of the anchor has brought renewed interest in our maritime past, and has sparked research into the Fortuna's past as well. The location of the Captain's baby who was born on and rescued from the ship in 1910 was a triumphant discovery, and she is planning to come from her home in Sicily to Ship Bottom, in September when the anchor from her father's ship is dedicated to our town. She expressed her joy "that so much is being done in a land so far away to honor the memory of her father, and is happy that two different countries can be joined by her father's place in history."

We know you cannot possibly be everywhere to join each and every town while it celebrates its cultural and historic heritage. We are certain that you, too, are proud of the role the sailing vessels played in the early development of our Country, and that you join us in spirit as we recognize the sacrifices of those men as we dedicate this anchor monument in their honor.

Sincerely,
Carole Bradshaw

#

The White House
Washington
September 4, 1985

Dear Ms. Bradshaw:

Thank you for your invitation for the President to attend the dedication of the Anchor from the *Fortuna* in Ship Bottom, New Jersey on September 28, 1985.

We appreciate your extending this opportunity to him. Unfortunately, I regret to write that due to the heavy demands on his schedule at that time he will be unable to be with you. However, he asked me to convey to you that he will be sending a special message for this important occasion.

With best wishes,
Sincerely,

FREDERICK J. RYAN, JR.
Director, Presidential Appointments and Scheduling

#

August 14, 1985
Saveria Fortunata Marina Adragna

Dear Saveria,

The story of the *Fortuna* and the "Fortuna Baby" appeared in our newspapers and many people have read it with much interest. Mrs. Carole Bradshaw, who discovered the Fortuna anchor off the shores of Ship Bottom, Long Beach Island in the state of New Jersey, has aroused great interest in the Fortuna shipwreck, especially among the Italian population in these parts.

The members of the Italian-American Club of Stafford Township in Manahawkin, N.J. near the area where the Fortuna anchor was found, would like to be part of the celebration at the Anchor Dedication and to financially support this lasting Italian memento in our part of the United States. Our Board of Trustees and members are planning a

Testimonial Dinner at our Italian-American Club in your honor on Friday evening, September 27, 1985.

We look forward to welcoming you for this festive occasion, and we feel certain that you will feel the warmth of the traditional Italian spirit in our midst as well as enjoying a delicious Italian dinner with us.

Edward A. Toriello
Chairman

#

End Notes

1. Taking a sounding: Often referred to as "heaving the lead," a sounding is taken when it is impossible to use a sextant or other navigational aid to fix a position. The sounding line is knotted at intervals measuring six fathoms apart and has a lead weight tied at the end. A hole in the weight is filled with tallow so that it picks up articles from the bottom of the ocean. The make-up of materials picked up in the tallow will indicate how dangerously close they may be to the shore.

2. Many letters and medals are still privately held by the families of the lifesavers. J. Horace Cranmer's letter and medal remain on display at the Beach Haven, New Jersey Public Library. This copy was on loan from the Mathews family, grandson of Caleb Conklin, Lifesaver.

3. The Lucy Evelyn: A schooner turned gift shop by Nat and Betty Ewer in 1949 on the boardwalk in Beach Haven, New Jersey. It burned to the ground in February 1972.

Bibliography

Bradshaw, Carole "Nonagenarian Recalls Fortuna's Misfortune," *SandPaper*, 11 July 1984, p. 31

Reddington, Linda "Remembering the Fortuna," *Beach Haven Times*, 16 Nov. 1983, p. 9 (as told to Carole Bradshaw by Lydie Neuendorf)

Nash, Charles Edgar *The Lure of Long Beach:* The Long Beach Board of Trade, 1936

LaVergne, TN USA
09 March 2010
175332LV00002B/8/P